THE ART OF FUND RAISING

THE ART
OF FUND RAISING

Third Edition

IRVING R. WARNER

FUND RAISING INSTITUTE
A Division of The Taft Group
Rockville, Maryland

First published 1975 by Harper & Row
Revised edition published 1984 by Bantam Books
Third edition published 1992 by Fund Raising Institute

Fund Raising Institute
A Division of The Taft Group
12300 Twinbrook Parkway, Suite 450
Rockville, Maryland 20852
(301) 816-0210

Printed in the United States of America

97   96   95   94   93   92   6   5   4   3   2   1

Library of Congress Catalog Card Number: 91-074044
ISBN 0-930807-27-8

Fund Raising Institute publishes books on fund raising, philanthropy, and nonprofit management. To request sales information, or a copy of our catalog, please write us at the above address or call 1-800-877-TAFT.

To Phala Ann

Contents

THE ART OF FUND RAISING

Preface

When World War II ended there were about 100,000 not-for-profit organizations to which you could make a contribution and get a federal tax deduction. In 1991 there are almost 1,000,000. In Chapter 2, you will find the startling statistics about the size of American charitable giving. You'll see that giving is not just a series of potluck dinners that raise $78.50 for the local Little League.

Another thing about fund raising that has changed dramatically in the last 40-odd years is professionalism. I was one of the first members of The National Society of Fund Raising Executives. Now the Society has more than 12,000 members. Other professional groups include the American Association of Fund-Raising Counsel, the Association for Healthcare Philanthropy, the Council for Advancement and Support of Education, and Independent Sector.

Some Universities have fund raising staffs of 150 or more. Everywhere you turn, there's a fund drive being directed by a professional, with an in-house publicity staff, photographers, and foundation grant-proposal writers.

Does the size of the fund raising enterprise with all that top notch professional competition scare you? Is it threatening? Are you afraid you and your really great project will not succeed? Take a good, deep breath and relax. Unless the American economy goes completely down the tubes, with civil war raging in the streets, you and your worthwhile program will find the money you need. I know, because I've worked with more than 175 organizations in the past 41 years, and I've watched hundreds of others, from newly hatched nestlings to full grown eagles go out into the cold, hard world and come home winners. I like the surgeons' line, "I never lost a patient on the table yet."

Neither will you, because you will do all the right things at the right time with the right people. If that sounds like Pollyanna, so be it. But you've done the right thing already by reading this book—not because there are miracles or magic tricks hidden here, but because you're not going off unprepared. Another reason you'll succeed is simply a matter of arithmetic. Americans have enough money to support anything they put their minds to. *When fund raising campaigns fail, it's not because there aren't enough potential donors, it's because there aren't enough askers.*

Be glad there's lots of competition out there clamoring for contributed dollars. They're educating the population to the needs of the people that are not being met by local, state or federal agencies. They are actually preparing your potential donor psychologically, and setting the stage for you. It's almost a variation of the law of physics: "Bodies in motion tend to stay in motion." Those who give to worthy programs tend to give to other worthy programs.

So, don't be put off by anything or anybody. If your campaign for $100,000 raises only $80,000, you didn't fail; you succeeded $80,000 in PHASE ONE. And the same would be true if your goal was $10,000,000.

I wish you 'good luck' with the sure knowledge that you probably won't need it because you're doing something worthy and your dedication will see you through.

Preface to First Edition

Sooner or later, whether you like it or not, you will be raising money for something. It may be the service club you belong to, your church, a national health campaign, the United Fund in your community, the school you went to, or some other cause you believe in. Fund raising has become part of our daily lives. Some estimates of the number of people involved as volunteers in fund raising range as high as 50 million.

I hope what I have to say about raising money will be valuable to the professional as well as the volunteer: to refresh him about things he already knows but may have forgotten; to remind him we are in the third largest dollar enterprise in America and we have a real obligation to our society.

But primarily this book is for the amateur volunteer. My respect and admiration for you are boundless. I rejoice with you when you succeed and I suffer with you through your failures. I see your hospitals and colleges and art museums and churches. I know about your homes for retarded children, I read the material from your think tanks, and I listen to your orchestras. Your free summer camps for needy children and your homes for the aged are monuments to your perseverance. You are there when catastrophe strikes or when a family needs help it can't get anywhere else.

Some volunteers are quite sophisticated and know more about fund raising than many professionals. More than a little of the material in this book I learned from you. Some of you are brilliant in several of the basic fund raising ideas but may need a little filling in here and there. The rest of you make up that remarkable group of people who are involved in noble causes, more or less playing it by ear, and, remarkably, succeeding—more or less.

Many of you come to see me because you don't know how to get started on your project. You are my special interest—you delight me. You are a blend of Don Quixote and Sancho Panza: you pursue impossible dreams with both feet firmly on the ground.

If this book gives you an idea or two or somehow makes you more effective and efficient, I shall have succeeded and your campaign will be the beneficiary.

Acknowledgments

To my mentor and friend Rudolf Flesch, deep thanks for everything he taught me, and for the examples he set.

To Zdenek Vanek whose encouragement was important to me.

I want to acknowledge, particularly, David Szonyi and Steve Shaw of the Radius Institute for their faith, persistence, and invaluable help.

And finally, to Seth Philip Warner who had the good sense to sleep most of the time this book was being written.

1

Before You Get Started

During the New York World's Fair of 1939 there was an exhibit with a primitive computer that answered mathematical questions. The computer was one of the first of its kind.

It answered questions instantaneously, just as computers do today. Back in 1939, people were not prepared for the speed with which they got the answers to complicated questions. Some of them were startled, others were frightened, and a few went into a state of temporary shock. To avoid any more problems, the exhibitor put in some meaningless extra relays so the answers wouldn't come out too fast.

I'm afraid I don't have any extra relays to delay the answer to the question "How do you raise money?"

So let me tell you straight out there's only one way to raise money: you have to *ask* for it. And, before you can be effective as an asker, *you* will have to *give* as much as you can afford.

Yes, you. This is the hardest thing I'm going to tell you to do. I risk offending you; that's not what you bought this book for, to be told you have to give first. Not only am I going to suggest you give first, but you will have to make a contribution that will be a real sacrifice for you. I'm not talking about the time and energy and thoughtfulness you are going to bring to your campaign. I take that for granted. I'm talking about dollars. Unless you are prepared to make the first gift and make it sacrificial, your campaign may not succeed.

Leadership carries responsibility. That's something we all know, and yet we sometimes forget it when it comes to community activity. When a group of patriots dressed as Indians dumped all that tea into Boston Harbor, they did it because of taxes. "No taxation without representation" was the slogan. In a fund raising campaign the slogan should be "No representation without taxation." If the leaders of a project don't make pace-setting gifts, why should others who are not that deeply involved give large sums? If you haven't convinced yourself, how will you convince me?

So here, in Table 1, is a giving chart for campaign leaders. If you give as much as I suggest, it will convince me and anybody else how important you think your project is.

TABLE 1
SUGGESTED SACRIFICIAL GIFTS FROM CAMPAIGN LEADERS

Net Annual Income After Taxes	$500,000 or more building fund or one-time campaign (3 years to pay)	$500,000 maintenance or annual campaign
Below $20,000	3 Weeks Pay	3–4 Days Pay
$ 25,000	$ 3,000	$500–800
$ 30,000	$ 5,000	$800–1,000
$ 50,000	$ 7,500	$1,000–1,500
$ 75,000	$10,000	$2,000–3,000
$150,000	$25,000 or more	$5,000–10,000

If the table doesn't fit your case, here's a rule of thumb that might. Figure out for yourself the largest gift you can possibly make to your campaign. Then, after you think about it for a while, if your gift won't force you to make any changes in your budget, it isn't enough.

Pretty steep? Remember I said sacrificial, not convenient. Leaders of a campaign must set high levels of giving. If you give more, you'll raise more. People in your bracket will rarely give more than you do because you're in charge of the campaign; they're just helping.

Does my table take unfair advantage of the rich? Not really. A bottle of milk costs the same for someone making $25,000 a year as it does for someone who makes $50,000. The more money you make, the more discretionary dollars you have left after you pay for necessities. Of course, the table is not for those who have unusual expenses that drain them constantly.

Building fund or one-time gifts are higher because the chances are you won't have to give again.

Please remember this is a *suggested* chart, a guide, not a commandment. It will probably be a sacrifice for you to give as much as I suggest, and if the sacrifice is too great, modify it. On the other hand, if I have succeeded in getting you to raise your sights, you have a better chance of raising the money you need.

Some years ago I consulted with a group that was concerned about a local community project in a big city. The first pledge to the campaign came from a board member. It was a pledge of $500 from a woman who earned her living by cleaning other people's houses in the rich part of the city. Her sacrifice inspired everybody on the board and it led the way to what is now a multimillion-dollar community health center in one of the worst slums in the United States. Five hundred dollars didn't do it, obviously, but it set the pace for all other gifts to the campaign. If a cleaning woman could give $500, what should a business tycoon give?

On another occasion I was called in by a group that wanted to do something about the uses and abuses of local coastal land. I asked the leaders of the group how much they had contributed to their project. They were shocked. They argued: "We are leading the campaign, we are bringing the truth to the community, we are spending our time setting up press conferences and preparing news releases. We didn't call you in to tell us what to do, we called you in to raise money for us."

They stoutly refused to make any gifts at all, let alone pacesetting contributions. I told them what I've just told you, but they didn't believe me. They floundered and died.

Now that the shock of these first pages is beginning to wear off, I'm going to ask you a number of questions— things you ought to think about before you get started on your fund raising campaign.

Have you done a feasibility study to find out your chances of success?

A feasibility study is a fancy term for asking a lot of people a lot of questions and doing a lot of reading on the subject you're interested in. No professional in his right mind would take on a client who needs a lot of money without doing one.

A feasibility study tests the water before you jump in. Starting on page 11 you will find a list of questions that can be asked during a study. You may want to add a few of your own or throw out some of mine. No two studies are alike because no two campaigns are alike. Yours may be local or national, for a new project or an old one, a campaign aimed at the members of your church or the rest of the community, or a combination of the two.

Chances are you have conducted an informal study of your own. See if you can recall what people said and then try to figure out if they really meant what they said. That's the key to a study, and it takes a good listener to hear the words underneath the words that tell you whether you can count on somebody or not.

If yours is a continuing project like an alumni campaign, you may not feel you need to do a study. Try one anyway. It's not a bad idea to talk to contributors about something besides money. You may discover hidden gripes that you can correct before they explode. You may find someone who is thinking about setting up a trust for your project but didn't know how to go about it. An hour-long animated conversation can bring up all sorts of things. During one interview I learned the man I was talking to had just been elected to the board of a large foundation, and yes, he would bring a proposal to the board for a grant to my client. He did and we got the money.

FEASIBILITY STUDY QUESTIONNAIRE

NAME _____ PHONES _____

ADDRESS _____ _____

OCCUPATION _____ DATE _____

1. When did you first become interested in the work of (your project)? Through whom?

2. Do you support any other agencies in (your project's) field with work and/or funds?

3. What is your judgment of how well the (your project) has carried out its stated aims?

4. What do you think of its short- and long-range objectives now, and its capacity to carry them out?

5. If (your project) were to vanish, what difference do you think its absence would make?

6. Are there specific projects you would like to see (your project) undertake?

7. Would you help finance that project or know where money for it might come from?

8. Are there any projects now in work which you disapprove of? Why?

9. If (your project) were to launch an effort to put itself on a solvent basis, could it count on your help—through a personal gift and asking others for their support?

10. Would you give small luncheon(s), tea(s), or dinner(s) at which the need for (your project's) programs and a review of work in progress were outlined, with a view toward getting financial support?

11. Would you consider making a bequest or creating an irrevocable trust for (your project)?

12. Would you serve on (your project's) board if you were asked?

13. Would you serve on a development committee?

14. Are there people we should talk to for support we might not know about? Who?

15. Would you act as our intermediary to reach them? Which ones?

16. Do you find a category below that fits your giving and getting potential for (your project)?

Size of Gift Over Five Years	Personal	Bequest or Deferred	From Others
$100,000+			
50,000			
25,000			
15,000			
10,000			
5,000			
2,500			
1,000			
Under $1,000			

17. Finally, and again in confidence, is there any advice you care to give the board or president on policies, priorities, programs, methods, staff, or anything else?

EVALUATION:

What we can expect.

When doing a feasibility study (sometimes called a *survey*) talk to as many donors and community leaders as you can. People have become a little cautious nowadays, so assure them they won't be solicited, and you'll have a better chance of getting an appointment when you want it.

Talk to them openly and directly about your project and *really* ask for their advice, guidance and opinions. You'll find that your study will do wonders for your project and will probably:

1. Show you the strengths and weaknesses of your organization and program.

2. Help you when you're ready to set a campaign goal.

3. Bring people closer to your project.

4. Prepare people for the campaign they know will follow.

5. Help identify leaders, prospects and suspects for your campaign.

6. Tell you what your community thinks of your program—what your image is.

I cannot recommend too strongly a study as your first step. It's like a medical examination. Would you allow a surgeon to operate on you without doing a thorough examination first? Neither would I, and you shouldn't *operate* on your community until you've examined it.

Do the large number of campaigns being run make you hesitate? Are you afraid they will reduce your chances or even kill you off?

Don't be afraid. The people who complain most bitterly about the volume of appeals they get usually don't give to anything. They're like the man who was visited by a committee from his alma mater for a contribution to the scholarship fund. He said, "Sure, it looks like I'm successful, but there are things you don't know. Like my sick mother and round-the-clock nurses; my sister's husband, who hasn't worked in four years and they have three kids; my father-in-law, who lost everything he had in a fire—I don't give *them* anything, so why should I give to you?"

One successful campaign in a community usually means others can be successful. People have to learn how to give; it's not an instinct. When they give to another campaign it has helped you by serving as a training exercise for your campaign. In the United States giving has jumped dramatically in recent years. Of course, most of that can be attributed to a growing economy, inflation and more money in the hands of more people. But don't overlook the value of the many sophisticated, professionally run campaigns that have trained people to give.

Years ago I had an assignment in Newark, New Jersey. The key to the campaign was a man who owned a furniture factory; if he became involved, success was guaranteed. There was one small catch: he never gave to anything. I stalked him for weeks. More to get me off his back than anything else, I think, he agreed to take part, reluctantly. As the campaign developed he began to understand how important his role was. He took it more and more seriously and increased his own gift several times. When it was finished, his sense of satisfaction was written all over him. In subsequent years he became a leader in several campaigns and a contributor to most of the community projects.

Miraculous? Unique? Hardly. He learned how to use his checkbook and how gratifying it was.

Would you be prepared to abort your campaign if it looked as though it couldn't succeed?

I'm talking about a new project, particularly. Your answer will be, "Of course." I'm not sure I believe you. I've seen it happen too many times—a group gets started, makes plans, falls on its face, gets up, starts again, gets no further than the first time, flops and starts again. That sounds pretty good; the old college try, never say die, if at first you don't succeed, the all-American spirit. Unfortunately, those old slogans don't apply. If you run a campaign correctly and it fails, there's a reason. And the reason is there's no support out there for your project. Not every problem has a solution and not every idea can raise the money it needs to fulfill it.

I once met with a group in the Midwest. They were trying to set up a private school for brain-injured children to provide the children with skills they might use later on to support themselves. It was a fine idea, and expensive.

But there was no federal program that could help with money, the state felt its institutions were sufficient to handle the problem, and the group didn't have enough influence to get the city to finance it.

They were hoping I could lead them to a millionaire who would give them everything they needed, because I was a professional fund raiser who must know lots of millionaires. I left them with advice on how to get started and a feeling they weren't going to take it.

That was a depressing example, so here's another. After a three-month feasibility study I wrote a report to the president of the organization. I didn't have the heart to tell him that *he* was the reason there probably wouldn't be any more money available to his project—he had offended or otherwise alienated every major source of money. Instead, I suggested that he prepare to retire and bring in another man to be trained as his replacement. He rejected my report, went ahead with plans of his own to raise money, failed, and finally closed down the program for lack of funds.

So, before you begin, bear in mind you may have to abandon your project, and be prepared to do it. Don't become a self-perpetuating failure.

Are you counting upon a windfall to see you through?

One of these days the world *will* come to an end. But down through the centuries, thousands of people have huddled all night on mountaintops only to be disappointed the next day when nothing happened. Unless you have a signed commitment from somebody, any thoughts about windfalls are nothing but fantasy.

I think it was a football coach who said, "Luck is the residue of good design." It's true in football and fund raising. A carefully planned campaign, well executed, will usually have a few pleasant surprises, but you can't anticipate them. When they happen, rejoice. If they don't happen and you have a well-planned campaign, you'll raise your money anyway.

Are there city, county, state, or federal funds earmarked for projects like yours?

There might be enough public funds available to you to make a campaign unnecessary. Or there might be matching funds—you get another dollar if you raise a dollar. Whatever the condition of public money may be, it's good to check into it before you start. If you start early you'll have time to get a proposal ready. Call or write your congressman, your state and city representatives. Tell them what you're doing and ask them to send you any appropriate legislation that looks as if it might help you.

Is there a national organization you ought to talk to?

If you're thinking about starting a group in your area to deal with a local problem, there just might be a national organization doing the same thing on a broader scale. You know about the many national health agencies that raise money to fight almost any disease you can name. If your group is thinking about doing something similar, get in touch with the national office. You may not want to affiliate with them, but they'll send you material that could be useful to you.

The national health organizations you hear about every day are only the tip of the iceberg. They have done an extraordinary job of making themselves well known. Other national or state organizations, however, may not be known to you. For example, there are national organizations for the prevention of blindness, for the rehabilitation of the blind, for Seeing Eye dogs, for training in braille, and for providing books in braille to the blind. It could be valuable to know whether you should affiliate, be independent, or simply abandon your project.

Have you been performing a service to the community or operating in the public interest without raising money and now find you need contributions to keep going?

Then you probably have directors or trustees who have never been called upon to give you money. They've helped you spend it and felt pretty good about it. Now you and they are faced with a moment of truth—the first money should come from the board, and Table 1 is a good way to start.

You may find some of your trustees suddenly too busy to come to meetings. Others will treat you as though you had bad breath. It happens. The chances are, however, you will retain a nucleus still dedicated to your project and you can build from them. Whatever you do, don't panic. Don't waste time scurrying around chasing rainbows. Treat your problem as though you were brand-new and start your project from ground zero. You're luckier than most groups because you have a history of service to the community, and though you're starting fresh, there's a backlog of goodwill you can call upon.

Have you been around a long time and it's getting harder and harder each year to raise money?

Before you start again this year, stop everything. Look at your past campaigns as though they were run by people out of the Stone Age. Hardening of the arteries is not restricted to people; organizations get it. How often have I heard leaders of annual campaigns talk about the need for "new blood," and then prevent the "new blood" from entering the body! They didn't mean a word they said because they had no intention of giving up their leadership. Many people adore the role of general in a campaign and wouldn't step down even if it meant losing the war.

So look closely at your campaign. Then turn it upside down if you have to. Abandon the old devices and dream up new ones; don't kick out the old generals, make them field marshals or something, but bring in those who have been waiting for a chance to do something and let them do it. Let me caution you about the chance of failure; it exists. But you'll never know unless you try, and meanwhile the generals get older. By the time you finish this book you may have discovered innovations you can use in your tired campaign. Don't be afraid to adapt them to your particular needs before you start.

Are you going into this project just because you happened to be elected fund raising chairperson of your organization?

That's bad. Your heart probably won't be in it and you'll do a perfunctory job. The best thing you can do is go back to the committee that elected you and try to get out of it. If they insist you keep the job or if you haven't the courage to quit, there's still hope.

Review the previous year's campaign, then cut last year's timetable in half. Insist that everything be done twice as fast. Compress the campaign into the shortest possible time span. Drive everybody nuts by insisting upon speed and more speed. Two good things will probably happen: the committee you're working with will do a better job because they won't be able to put things off, and you'll get rid of your job more quickly.

I'm reasonably sure that some of these questions will have a direct bearing on your project. Think about them carefully before you start. Talk them over with others in your group and get their reaction.

Don't leave your common sense behind you when you

discuss your project. That's not a piece of idle advice: some people change completely when they take part in a community activity. All the things they know about, all the good business methods, all the common sense they have acquired over the years is abandoned because they think business and philanthropy function under different sets of rules. Not so. But it's a hard lesson to learn.

Just recently, trustees of several major universities have begun to look into their endowment funds to see if they could increase income to keep pace with rising costs. Some of the things they found appalled them. As businessmen they knew there were many safe investments available at relatively high rates of return. What they found in the endowment portfolios were investments dating back many years and returning astonishingly low interest. These old investments had also been made by businessmen—but businessmen who had left their good sense outside the doors of the boardroom.

So, before you get started, promise yourself to use every tool at your command, including your good common sense.

2

The Art of Fund Raising

Fund raising *is* an art. Comparing it to painting, sculpture, or music may be carrying it too far, so let's try cooking. Almost anybody can prepare a nourishing meal, even if it means opening a dozen cans to do it. Anyone who can read can follow a recipe from a cookbook. Fund raising has recipes, too. It has techniques and practices you can learn just as you can learn to fold an egg into batter, or how to stuff a turkey. You'll never become an artist if you don't master them, but you'll never become an artist if all you learn are techniques to which you become a slave.

Samuel Jackson Snead, the golfer who won more tournaments than any other professional in the history of the sport, changed his putting stance drastically late in his career. His old winning stance didn't work any more. And if something I tell you doesn't work, discard it. Nothing in this book is a natural law. In this inexact art the apple that falls from the tree doesn't always land on the ground.

That's what's so much fun about fund raising. It can't be written as a formula and it can't be put into a computer, as some of my colleagues have tried to do.

Some years ago I started to teach myself how to cook. I was terrible. Purely by accident I watched Julia Child's television program on cooking and I will always be grateful to that great lady. She was preparing *coq au vin.* Twice Mrs. Child dropped the chicken on the kitchen floor. Twice she bent down, picked it up, dusted it off, and proceeded. In that one program I learned a great lesson; I was never again intimidated by a recipe or ingredients.

And you shouldn't be intimidated by me or the techniques in this book. I've dropped a couple of chickens myself in more than forty years as a professional.

Now that we understand each other, let's take a brief look at philanthropy in America. It may help toward a new perspective on giving money away.

Here's how big philanthropy in America is:

General Motors is the largest corporation in the United States. In 1989 Americans gave away 27 times as much money as General Motors earned.

In 1989 Americans gave away 32% more than the incomes of the radio, television and motion picture industries combined, and we gave away over 3 times more money than all the mining companies in the country made. That includes coal, silver, gold, copper, lead, uranium, etc., etc.

Not impressed yet? How about this?

In 1989 Americans gave away almost twice as much money as the entire budget of the Commonwealth of Australia.

In 1989 Americans gave away $114.7 BILLION. That's $114,700,000,000.*

However, in 1989 personal income in the United States amounted to more than $4.3 *trillion.* So, if Americans had given away as much as 3% of what we made, we would have given away $131.5 billion—or almost $17 billion more than we actually contributed. That additional money could have provided $20 worth of food every day for a year for

---

*American Association of Fund-Raising Counsel, *Giving USA* (New York: 1990). Income figures are the latest available at this writing.

2,330,000 people. Or, a $4,000 scholarship for just about every high school or college student in the United States.

What I am saying boils down to this: Americans are generous, but we don't give away as much as we could. How many people do you know who give away the biblical tithe, 10 percent? How many people do you know who have changed their life styles because of the amount of money they gave away to worthy causes?

So you see there's plenty of room for your new project and even more for your proven older one.

If you were to ask me why people as generous as Americans don't give away more, I would have to confess I don't know. But I do know that among the reasons campaigns don't raise as much money as they could, none is more important than the fact that *most people hate to ask other people for money face to face.* Almost every fund raising device I have ever heard of was invented to ease the agony of asking somebody for money.

Everybody has a very personal attitude about money. Some people flaunt it, others are embarrassed by it, some are outwardly indifferent toward it, but almost everybody hates to ask other people for it. And you may be one of them. If I'm wrong, you are that rare breed who is the delight of ministers and college presidents, YMCA directors and chairpersons of local health appeals.

If I'm right, and you hate it, here is what probably goes through your mind: It's degrading. You'd rather give the money yourself than have to beg for it. Sometimes you do give it yourself if it's not a large sum. You can't think of anything that embarrasses you more than asking a stranger to contribute money. When it comes to asking friends, the thought of it makes you cringe. Right? Well, you will have to do some hard thinking but your fear is curable. Because that's what it is, fear.

Why is asking for money degrading? What goes through

your mind when you contemplate raising money? This isn't intended to be armchair psychotherapy, but your fear has no basis in reality. It stems from your attitude toward money. No two people feel precisely the same about it. It's among the most emotionally charged words in our vocabulary.

It took you years to arrive at your present feeling about money and I can't change it, but maybe I can get you to examine your attitudes and help you to be more comfortable with them.

For seven years, starting in the late sixties, I was counsel to a small New England college with a phenomenal record for raising money. The major reason for the record was the college president, a man unlike any I had ever met. While my role with the college as counsel covered a multitude of chores, the most productive and most rewarding was arranging luncheons for the president with one potential giver at a time. Just the three of us. Within minutes after sitting down to lunch the president invariably said, "This is going to be the most expensive luncheon you ever ate." Of course, many hours of careful research went into every appointment. He was never turned down in my presence.

He was honest, open, and direct. There were no cute ploys, no innuendos, no hints or beating around the bush. The giver always knew what was happening and appreciated that he was being treated honestly. The president was never at a loss for a new and different approach to the subject of money. He didn't need any. He talked about the school and its needs, and asked for a specific amount of money to meet part of those needs. While he didn't always get as much as he asked for (he usually pegged his request about 25 percent higher than my estimate), he always came away with a handsome gift and the respect of the giver.

Now back to you. "Sure," you say, "a brilliant college

president, hours of research on the prospect, and you expect me to do the same thing?" My answer is yes. You don't have to be brilliant to be honest, and anybody can find out things about other people if he tries.

You *know* you're not asking for yourself when you solicit a contribution. You *know* the cause is good. You *know* if you don't do it, it won't get done.

Let's turn it around. How do you feel when somebody asks *you* for a contribution? Do you hate him? Are you afraid of her? Do you feel guilty, ashamed, diminished? Do you feel those things when *you* do the asking? Do you feel the person you're asking will think you're not as nice as you would like him to think? Does asking lower the image you have of yourself?

These questions may sound simple, but they're hard to ask ourselves. They probe deeply into areas some people don't want to examine. The more you insist the reason you don't like fund raising is because you just don't like to ask for money, the more important the questions become. You cannot let yourself off the hook by saying you don't like it because you don't like it.

Some years ago I called on a wealthy influential man we needed as chairman for a campaign. I told him, "Mr. Sforza, fate has put you in a position to be of enormous service to your community." Mr. Sforza was sold. He couldn't deny the truth. He *was* the best man for the job.

Fate has put *you* in the same position. You have good intentions, you have a conscience, you want to help others. Don't be afraid, don't feel intimidated, don't feel guilty. By asking others you are giving *them* an opportunity to take part in something greater than themselves. You give them a feeling of accomplishment. They feel better. Don't you feel good when you give to a good cause? Share the feeling with others. They'll think more of you for it, not less.

In the back of your mind there is still a little doubt. "Okay," you say, "maybe I can get myself to ask the average person, somebody like me, but what about our local millionaire? How can I presume to put the bite on him for our hospital?"

It's a problem. Most of us are in awe of very rich people. They don't have to be very, very rich, just a lot richer than we are. So here we have a double problem: to overcome our fear of asking for money and our fear of people with great wealth.

Don't be fooled, the very rich are *not* very different. They do give away a greater percentage of their income, on the average, than those of us with less money. Internal Revenue Service figures of the last twenty years prove it. But that's because they have more money to give away.

Rich people are usually well educated, so there is a good chance they will understand the need for the money you ask for. It makes your job *easier*. While you may have examples to show I'm wrong, I have found the very rich often have a deep sense of obligation to the community.

So strip away the fear and you can raise money for almost anything. And you'll enjoy it. Fund raising can be among the most satisfying things you can do.

I would give a pledge card to a dragon if I thought he would sign it, and that's how you should feel.

So before we go on to other things, here's my definition of the art of fund raising: You raise money when you ask for it, preferably face to face, from the smallest possible number of people, in the shortest period of time, at the least expense.

3

Getting Started:
The Five C's

Alliteration is a lovely 5-syllable word that means 're-
peating the first letter of a series of two or more words,' as
in, "Fifty-four forty or fight."* I use it often in my classes
on fund raising because it is a useful tool as a mnemonic
device. [Mnemonic is another charming, many-syllabled
word, silent first M, which means 'memory aid.']

There are five basic elements in a fund raising campaign. All of them are necessary, and to help you remember them, I've made them alliterative—they all begin with
the letter C. The elements are Case, Constituency, Chairperson, Committee, Counsel. Later in the book I go into
greater detail on all of them, but now let's take a quick
look at the campaign elements so you will see how they fit
together in a neat package.

The Case, of course, is the compelling reason for your
prospects to contribute to your cause.

The Constituency is the group to whom you will bring
your Case, your prospective contributors.

The Chairperson is the one who brings the Case to the
Constituency. The Chairperson also recruits the Committee who help bring the Case to the Constituency.

*The 1845 slogan and threat to England, during the presidency of James K.
Polk when the U.S. claimed all of the Northwest Territory as the country's
Manifest Destiny. It didn't work.

The Counsel is either you who have taken the interest and the time to read this book, or the executive director of the organization, or a volunteer who rides herd on everything, or a professional fund raising person who co-ordinates every aspect of your campaign.

If all this sounds like a kindergarten mnemonic song, good! I want you to memorize the 5 C's, and as your campaign takes shape and begins to move ahead, go back often to the 5 C's and make sure they are all in place and you are doing what you are supposed to do.

All the elements are necessary, but some are more necessary than others. And the most important element, the vital ingredient in your campaign is leadership.

So let me tell you about some chairmen and chairwomen I have known. I won't use their real names, but I hope they recognize themselves. I'd like them to know how much they taught me and how grateful I am.

Ben Proling was cash collection chairman of a campaign I worked on several years ago. We had hundreds of thousands of dollars in pledges but we were having some trouble converting them into dollars. Letters and reminders didn't seem to work.

Ben was dedicated to the project and had made a substantial gift to it, considering the size of his metals fabricating plant. We reviewed the lists of people who had not redeemed their pledges and discussed possible reasons why they hadn't. Ben wouldn't accept any explanation short of outright catastrophe for a man not to honor a pledge made in good faith. It was beyond his ability to understand that everybody wasn't as honest as he was. But he was intelligent enough to know he would get some brilliant excuses unless he developed a foolproof collection method. And he did.

Here's how it worked: He would call a man on the list and talk about the state of the economy, the weather, and business conditions in general. He would suggest that he had thousands of dollars in cash in his office safe begging for a place to be invested. Couldn't a use be found for, say, $10,000? Surely with the current money crunch $10,000 would come in handy and Ben would love to help a fellow supporter of our project. No? You have no need now for $10,000? Really? Then wouldn't this be the right time to pay off your pledge? I can send my driver right over to pick up your check! Every call was successful.

Heavy-handed? Ben didn't think so. The people he called were his peers; they were members of the same club and their wives saw each other socially and worked on local charities together. What Ben did was to remind them of a moral obligation and save them the embarrassment of having to invent excuses or lying.

I asked Ben what he would have done if someone had taken him up on his offer of $10,000 to invest. "I'd have given it to him," he said.

Perry Wilkens was chairman of a public-interest project I worked on. Perry was almost frighteningly articulate. He could take a concept of almost impenetrable complexity and make it clear to anyone. He had one other quality in greater abundance than anyone I had ever known before—he refused to be turned down. He took it as a personal failure if he couldn't convince everybody he talked to that our project deserved support. When he met someone for the first time, he got the person's address and phone number. He found out what his hobbies were. The *next day* he would send the man a note with a little information about our project, a clipping about the prospect's hobby, or a book, or an invitation to a tennis game—something always went with the note. Within about six weeks the prospect was getting five- and six-page letters every other day (each different!) about our campaign and why it needed his support. It soon became apparent that

Perry wouldn't give up, so capitulation was the only way out. I should add that in most cases Perry's arguments convinced the prospect, who then contributed willingly. When that happened, Perry would have access to the prospect's list of friends and business associates and the process would begin all over again. At one time I estimated Perry was in almost daily touch with more than two hundred potential contributors. It was awe-inspiring.

Perry Wilkens explained what he did and why in these terms: His project was a necessary one. It had to be supported by contributions because it was outside the area of any government or foundation grants. He was doing the prospect a favor by exposing him to the project. The prospect would thank him ultimately. They usually did.

Hettie Robbins was the social leader of her group in a major U.S. city in the South. Her New Year's Eve party was the social event of the year. But lest you think she was simply a party-thrower, she was also the moving force behind several projects in the community, and I had the privilege of working with her one year when she was chairwoman.

After going over various campaign plans, we decided the kickoff would be a small dinner for top prospects. At the dinner we hoped to solicit their pledges for the year and recruit them for Hettie's committee. You can see that our campaign would succeed or fail depending upon how many men attended the dinner. We had six weeks to do everything and any delay would be costly.

Hettie invited seventy men to the kickoff. When regrets outnumbered acceptances 3 to 1, Hettie was upset. How dare they invent lame excuses for not coming? Did they think because she was a woman they could ignore her and their community responsibility? She would tolerate neither bad manners nor irresponsibility and she intended to do something about it. She did.

My phone rang incessantly for two days. Men who had said they weren't coming to the kickoff dinner called me to ask what in hell was going on. What was Hettie trying to do, wreck their marriages? "Get her off my back, tell her I'm coming to the dinner."

What Hettie did was to phone the wives of the men who had refused her invitation. She told them how important the project was and how essential their husbands' attendance would be. She reminded the wives of her long memory—people who refused one invitation from Hettie rarely got another.

Sixty-eight men attended the dinner—only because the other two were out of the city on legitimate business and were forgiven. The campaign was a triumph.

Blackmail? Bad taste? Perhaps. Hettie reasoned this way: "We have a very nice community; we have fun together and we share many blessings, but a community should share other things, too. I reminded them of that."

Ben Proling, Perry Wilkens, and Hettie Robbins are as different from each other as people can be. But in their differences are striking similarities. They share a zest for living, their ideals have not corroded into cynicism, they do things because things need doing, they don't trip over their own sense of self-importance, and they are perfect chairpersons.

So all hail to the chief, the chairperson. If you've got the right one, he's the most important asset in your campaign. If he's the wrong one, he can drive you straight up the wall of a padded room. You can succeed in your objectives without the perfect chairperson, but you will probably bomb if you pick the wrong one for the job.

Take your time before you offer anybody the chairmanship. Even though yours may be way down the list of things people want to associate with, don't peddle the chairmanship around—the man you could get may turn you down because he wasn't asked first.

Who is the one you want?

He/She is rich. If it's inherited wealth, he's third generation: if he's a businessman, he has more accounts payable than receivable. That means lots of people depend upon him for their living. He buys things from them, and when he pays, they make a profit. The owner of a department store who buys furniture, clothing, appliances, and hardware from factories would be a better choice than the Chevrolet dealer, who may be rich but has to sell his cars to you and me.

He/She has what the pros call "clout," influence with other rich people that goes beyond social contact. Clout may be political, so that prospective donors would give for whatever favors they think they may get in return. Clout usually is financial; by giving to your ideal chairperson, donors protect a business contact with him or try to get one. *Clout* and *rich* almost always go together and they are the most valuable attributes a chairperson can have.

He/She is generous to lots of causes. While it may be valuable for your chairman to have an identity as "Mr. Hospital of Springfield," donors will resent him unless he takes part in other community activities. "Mr. Boy Scouts of Springfield" won't make an adequate gift to the hospital unless Mr. Hospital makes an adequate gift to the Boy Scouts. Two quick side notes: (1) What's the good of the two chairmen trading gifts when they could just as easily give to their own campaigns? Because it will have an effect on other donors to the "competition" whom you might solicit. Plus there are important campaigns and *very* important campaigns. If yours is a *very* important one, the chairman of the competition can be asked for more money than your chairman would have to give him. (2) Clout overcomes most obstacles. If your chairman has more clout than theirs, you'll come out ahead most of the time.

He/She is well liked. If your chairperson is well liked he can attract people to your project on that basis. It would be a good beginning, and the value of what you're doing becomes the clincher.

He/She is a true believer in the project. The more he believes, the more money he'll give to it, the more convincing he'll be in asking others, the more enthusiasm he'll generate— and enthusiasm is infectious.

He/She is well organized. He'll be able to put together a campaign that has a logical beginning, middle, and end. He'll allocate his time appropriately and won't be out of the city when you need him most. He'll do what has to be done because that's his style, and he'll see to it that others do their jobs.

He/She is a good speaker. He'll be able to convince groups that what you're doing is important. You won't flinch when he's interviewed by the mass communications media.

He/She is fearless. He'll talk to anybody about your campaign. He'll stay with you under pressure from the outside and the inside—from the community or your own group.

That's your perfect chairman, a man for all seasons and reasons. If you find him, protect him. Be sure he stays out of drafts and takes his vitamin pills. He's worth looking for and waiting for. I once waited six months for a man we needed as chairman. The president of the organization fumed with impatience, but I held fast. The potential chairman's wife had recently died and I knew he had been devastated; but he would recover. He did and the campaign succeeded.

Perfect chairmen are rare. I would have said nonexistent except that I have worked with a few. Your chances of finding one are slim, so you should be prepared to settle for less than perfect.

Let's review the necessary conditions for chairperson and see where you might compromise.

Rich and clout. I said they usually go together, but let's separate them. You could compromise on rich provided you don't go much below "very comfortable" if your campaign is for a relatively small amount. The only absolute substitute for rich is "extraordinary visibility," somebody like Dwight Eisenhower when he was alive, if he would do it—I mean work at the chairmanship. You can adjust the "visibility" to your own community if your project is local. But I hope you understand what I mean by visibility—*everybody* knows and likes him, respects him, admires him, and would automatically be interested in anything he did. Since having extraordinary visibility is rarer than being rich, stay with rich.

Clout rates almost exactly equal to rich with the balance needle tipping a tiny bit toward clout. If a man is rich but has no influence with other people, the most you can expect is a good contribution. If he has a great deal of influence but not a great deal of money, he'll get money from many sources. There are no rules here. You'll have to determine for yourself the extent of the clout, so take your time and get as much information as you can about your prospective chairman and the amount of influence he really has.

Generous to others. Not vital, but a good thing generally. If you're going out on a community-wide campaign it becomes more important. You could do without it, but it wouldn't do any harm to suggest to your chairman he give to other things, too. I conducted a campaign in which the chairman gave $100,000 to our institution and much smaller gifts to other causes. We had great difficulty with potential big donors who were interested in the other causes, but the chairman we had was the best one we could get.

Well liked. Vital to a community-wide campaign, imperative to a closed-constituency campaign (church, local alumni). Avoid a chairman like the one who was visited in the hospital by a member of his board. The board member told him, "We had a meeting last night and someone proposed a resolution wishing you a speedy recovery. I'm pleased to tell you the resolution passed seven to five."

True believer. This is not as important as you might think, but it's great when you get it. You'll probably have more success recruiting a true believer than a lukewarm one. Remember, however, that true believers can be unpredictable—their enthusiasm can carry them off in directions you may not want to go. I had one as a chairman about ten years ago. He was a dynamo. He found prospects I didn't know existed, and got money from them. But he was usually at odds with the other members of the board and often proposed methods and techniques that were too expensive or couldn't work. If I had it to do over again, I'd still take him, however. He taught me a lesson I'll pass on to you here, even though it's out of sequence: Never, ever assume a prospect won't give, no matter what his previous history, philosophy, or record of giving may have been.

Well organized. Down the list of vital attributes, especially if he has help in organization. If your chairperson lacks this asset, it's your job to provide it, whether you're pro or amateur.

Good speaker. Nice to have for community-wide campaigns, but somebody else can take over for him if necessary. Least important of the qualities you should look for.

Fearless. High up on the priority list. A weak chairperson can call off a campaign at the slightest sign of resistance, and he has the authority to do it—you gave it to him. He can find resistance in strange places, like the person who turns him down for a contribution. Or possible competition from another campaign for a totally different cause. Or the negative state of the economy. Avoid the weak chairman at all costs. That's a nice piece of advice, but how can you tell in advance if he's strong or weak? Did he ever head a campaign before? If he did, ask the professional involved or some of the people he worked with; ask how he handled crisis situations. Or check with his personal and business friends—find out if he stays with his convictions in politics, business, child rearing, etc. In short, check him out any way you can and then hope for the best.

Your chairperson will have to be given policy-making authority. If he's not already on the board of your project, put him on. The more important he feels, the harder he will work.

If you think I'm stressing the importance of the chairman beyond his real value, you're wrong. He's so important to you that a full-length book about the finding, recruiting, care, and feeding of chairmen could be written. He's as important to you as the chief executive officer is to a corporation, because that's what he really is in your case.

What about honorary chairmen, co-chairmen, or the big-name chairman that other campaigns always seem to get?

Abraham Lincoln was supposed to have told the story about the man who was being ridden out of town on a rail. Asked if he had any final words, the man looked around, saw the whole town assembled to watch, and said, "If it wasn't for the honor of the thing, I'd just as soon walk."

Honorary chairmen are about as valuable as the size of the gifts they make. The value they *might* have comes in when you're a relatively unknown project and the honorary chairman is well known enough to lend credibility to you. Or if you've got a current chairman who's stepping down and you don't know what else to do with him, make him honorary chairman. But don't waste your time actively recruiting one.

Co-chairmen, however, are a different proposition. The absence of the ideal chairman, that paragon of all virtues, may lead you to two or perhaps three men who have, among them, the qualities of the ideal chairman. Or when you recruit your ideal man and he hesitates because he's genuinely modest or reluctant to take on sole responsibility, offer him the co-chairmanship.

The big-name chairman of the other campaign may not be everything he seems to be, unless he was recruited using our guidelines. Too often the big-name chairman never gets his hands dirty in the campaign. The people who recruited him gave away everything they wanted and needed in a chairman just to get his big-name value, whatever that might be. Be content with your compromise chairman if you get him the right way.

And here's how you get him. After you review the qualities he should have, make a list of the potential chairmen of your choice, most desirable one first down to somebody you can live with last.

Don't simply pluck names out of a hat. There should be a reasonable connection between the man and the project. Maybe he's already a member of your group, a close friend or business contact of a group member, a known advocate of what you're trying to do or sympathetic to it. Somehow you should have a hook to your potential chairman or forget about him. He'll turn you down and that will set you back in your schedule and your morale, and word may get out to make it tougher to approach your next candidate.

Choosing the right chairperson is where fund raising sometimes approaches an art. Your evaluations and diagnoses are critical. The ability to find the right man to take the job separates the short-order cook from the Escoffier.

Call the first person on your list and make an appointment to see him. Avoid telling him (or her) why you want to see him, if possible. Explain it's about something important enough to justify lunch or an hour in his office or his home.

Never, never try to recruit him (or her) by mail. The perfect chairman is not sitting around waiting to be asked. He needs to be convinced, and he has more reasons to turn you down than you can imagine. If you give him the chance to think about your offer by sending him a letter, he'll have enough time to sit back and dictate a masterful refusal. He can refuse face to face, too, but it's harder.

If your choice puts you off when you call, try to nail down some date and time he can see you. Be firm; polite, of course, but firm. Get an appointment.

When you see him (or her), don't go alone. Bring at least one other person with you, preferably two. Don't barge in with a committee of ten. And don't bring just anybody. Think carefully about the makeup of the visiting group. Here's where your artistic ability comes in again. Do you bring the chief of staff of the hospital or some bright young surgeon? The minister of the congregation or the choirmaster? The banker who's a member of your group or the mother of an afflicted child? Or both? If you've done your homework on your choice of chairperson, it will be easier to figure out who the askers should be.

Be relaxed when you visit, but be considerate of your candidate's time. Have all your arguments ready. Tell him everything about your project and why he should be chairperson, and tell it as concisely as possible. If you're going to have professional help, tell him so. Keep the conversation rolling by giving the others in your group the chance to make telling arguments on their own.

Tell him how much time he would be expected to put in. Give him the names of others in your group who are going to work with him and when you expect to finish. Tell him how much the inner group has pledged so he'll know how much money is expected of him.

If you sense he might accept but is reluctant to take on

the sole responsibility, suggest a co-chairmanship, but only if you're sure he'll refuse without it. Bring out your list of potential chairmen and let your man recruit his own co-chairman from the list—that will be his first official act as your top man. Again, if you've researched your candidate properly, he'll have enough clout to recruit the help he thinks he needs.

Why should your choice of chairperson accept? You're asking him to give up time and money, put his reputation on the line, and assume another responsibility he doesn't need. Because you convinced him. In your approach, you combined the cleverness of Ben Proling, the determination of Perry Wilkens, and the morality of Hettie Robbins. Could anyone resist?

In most cases your choice will ask for time to think about the offer. Try to avoid it. Do everything you can to get an answer then and there. Remember, this is your one best chance at him; you may not get another. Take your clue from the used-car salesman who will do anything to keep customers from leaving the lot, because he knows they might not come back. If that sounds harsh, boorish, aggressive, abrasive, remember your project. Is it important to you? Besides, everything I've told you can be done in good taste; part of the art of fund raising is the art of gentle persuasion.

You've done everything right, you've been meticulous in your research and persuasive in your arguments and just perfect in everything, and your choice of chairperson says no anyway. What do you do?

It happens all the time, to beginners, talented amateurs, and pros. So don't feel crushed, because there's still a lot you can do as long as you are sitting there with your man and have his attention.

The strategy is like the scorched-earth policy the Russians used in World War II during the Nazi invasion. As the Nazis advanced, the Russians defended every step along the way as well as they could. When defeat was imminent, they withdrew to new defense positions and burned everything behind them. Do the same thing. When he says no and you're sure he means it, drop it. Retreat to a new position and don't bring up the chairmanship again. Take out your list of potential chairmen, show it to him, and ask for his help in recruiting your next choice. If he suggests another name, get him to agree to work with you in recruiting. If that position fails, retreat once again. Ask him if he'll serve on your committee. If that fails, ask for a contribution from his foundation or his company. And finally, when all else fails, ask him directly for a pledge to help you kick off your campaign, then go out and recruit your next choice.

After you recruit your chairperson, the next step is putting together a committee.

Your committee starts with your inner group. They will be the support your chairman must have. You can and should add to your committee those other choices for chairman you researched so carefully. Recruit them the same way you recruited your chairman, only this time you have his added persuasion so your job will be that much easier.

On page 41 is a rating scale that you can use to tell whether the people you're getting or the people you've got are as good as they could be for your organization. Use it as a way to check, but don't become a slave to it.

A word here about advisory committees and letterhead committees. If you are sure you need the credibility well-known names on your letterhead may give you, go after them. But I have more than a sneaking suspicion many famous people don't know about 50 percent of the letterheads they're on.

Don't create a letterhead committee just because everybody else has one. Their reasons may not apply to you. But if you do, get acceptances in writing. It's a law in some states or it may save you embarrassment if your famous name forgets he said yes and complains about having his name used. Advisory boards are useful if they *really* advise or if they serve as spokesmen when you need them. They may be helpful in recruiting your chairman or bolstering his faith in the campaign once you get him.

RATING SCALE FOR BOARD MEMBER (TRUSTEE) OF NONPROFIT ORGANIZATION/INSTITUTION WITH FUNDING NEEDS FROM PUBLIC AND FOUNDATION SOURCES (SCALE FROM 0 TO 10 BY ½ INCREMENTS WITH 10 AS BEST OR MOST DESIRABLE)

1. Professional standing in the organization's field (medicine, education, art, etc.)   _____

2. Personal prestige, credibility, and visibility   _____

3. Professional skills needed by the organization (accounting, law, investment, building, etc.)   _____

4. Ability and *willingness* to contribute dollars. Multiply by 2   _____

5. Ability and *willingness* to solicit others. Multiply by 2   _____

6. Political influence   _____

7. Geographic diversity   _____
   0 if 20% of board is from same area   Score only if
   10 if no one on board is from same area   relevant to
      organization

8. Promotional potential (via mass communications media) _____

9. Promotional potential (via country clubs, service organizations, business associations, etc.) _____

10. Age and past experience on other boards (value judgment on board needs of youth or experience or perfect balance of both) _____

11. Attitude: loyalty to organization, to its aims and goals (0 = cool, 10 = avid support) _____

12. Wisdom, intelligence, and leadership qualities and *willingness* to apply these qualities to board membership _____

13. Current active service on other boards: _____
    0 boards = 0
    1 other board = 5
    2 other boards = 10
    3 other boards = 7½
    4 or more other boards = 0

A score of 80 or more is good.

So you have a chairman and a committee and you're ready to roll. Not quite. But you have the most important ingredients of your campaign recipe. About the oldest cliché in fund raising is the one that says, "People give to people." It's also the truest. I hate to say it, but if my *sole* purpose was to raise money, I'd rather have the right chairman and committee for *any* campaign than the wrong ones for the most noble purpose on earth.

Most pros would tell you to start with what we call the *case*—the arguments supporting your project. My advice is to start with people. Without them you can't get anything done, but with them you can do almost anything. With the right combination of people I helped guide a mental health facility in the Midwest to $23 million in 1982. Another of my clients raised $200,000 for a project as important as the one in the Midwest, but with a chairman and committee not as strong.

Don't misunderstand me; your case is important if you hope to raise money and you should spend the time and money it takes to make it persuasive and compelling.

Here's what you have to do. Pretend you're writing a letter to a friend explaining your project and you have only one sheet of paper left. Avoid flowery language and superlatives. Compress it, squeeze out the water. You'll have plenty of opportunity to expand later, but now you need a tight, brief, short, succinct. . . . You're beginning to get the idea.

While every case may be different, all have the same objective: to make it easier for you when you ask for a contribution. Don't ever expect the written word, the brochure, the book, the architect's drawings, or the photographs to take the place of direct asking. The printed case is a tool, no more. As a tool it has to be useful, not fancy. In your kitchen you don't need gold-handled knives to cut bread.

When you have your one-page case written, it should tell your friend what your project is trying to do, why it's important to get it done, and how much it will cost. If you can't write it yourself, get somebody else in your group to write it, *alone*. It should be the work of one person, not a committee. By now you must surely have heard the comedian's definition of a camel—a horse designed by a committee.

Additional pages in your case can have photographs, graphs and charts, drawings, lists of committees and chairmen, and a financial breakdown of need and costs, like an annual report from a corporation. It should be well designed, but not to the point that design overpowers content. You might have two versions printed: one small enough to fit into an ordinary letterhead envelope you can buy at any stationer's, and one larger to leave with people.

Your printed case may cost a lot of money, but it should not look as though it did. No fancy leather books, please. No shiny, coated paper everybody knows costs oodles of money. Good taste, that most difficult term to define, shall be your guide.

The printed case is not nearly so important to your prospects as it is to you and the people in your inner, working group. That may sound strange, but it's true. Your prospect may look at it, turn it over, browse through it, and *maybe* read it from beginning to end. On the other hand, you will fondle it, gaze at it, and see if your name is spelled right. You'll devour it, and you should. It has transformed your whole project from a fantasy in your mind to the reality of the printed page. Your hospital exists! You can smell the fresh air of the summer camp! And you are proud.

Some of my colleagues place a great deal of importance on the printed case. I don't. A good, well-written, persuasive printed brochure is nice to have, and you should have one if it makes you feel good. You should have one if your campaign is large enough in dollars and numbers of people. Use good judgment and remember a brochure is only as effective as the person who follows up and asks for the contribution.

Any good printing company will be glad to send you several samples of brochures to use as references. Take advantage of them; that's what they're in business for and they won't mind a bit. Collect brochures from other campaigns that solicit you and compare them. See which fits your project best. Don't be afraid to adapt style or format if it's exactly what you had in mind in the first place.

Shop around for a printer. Prices vary. But be sure the estimates you get are for the same grade of paper, the same number of brochures, etc. If labor unions are a possible source of money or labor union people are important inner family members, by all means use a union printer. See to it that the union "bug" or symbol appears on your letterhead and brochure.

Don't expect a printer to work for nothing because you are a charitable organization. If you can find one who will, great. The most you should expect would be a discount because you're nonprofit. Once you find a printer who seems right for you, tell him he will do all of your printing in the future, but remind him you'll expect a lower price for your work in the future. He'll usually agree because he won't have to bid for your printing. Printers build in a cost factor for bidding because they don't get every job they bid for, and somebody has to pay for the time they put in for jobs they don't get.

So you're just about ready for a campaign. You have a chairman, a committee, and a printed case statement. Your inner family has made sacrificial gifts. Unless the roof caves in, your campaign will probably succeed. But finish reading the book anyway, just for the fun of it.

4

Goals and Costs

Most Americans are what psychologists call "goal oriented." We seem to do better and work harder when we have an objective to work for. It's part of our character. Remember how you crammed before exam week?

The career and life goals we set for ourselves tell much about us, and in a fund-raising campaign, your goal tells your prospects a lot about you, as you will see. But more often than not, the people in charge of a campaign aren't fully aware of the significance of the goal and how much care they should take in setting it. They may not even be aware there are four types of goals you can set for a campaign: less than you think you can raise; more than you think you can raise; about the amount you think you can raise; and *no* goal.

THE LOW GOAL. Why would anybody set a goal lower than he thought he could achieve? Because it's impressive when you surpass your goal. The board, the committee, and the community get the idea that you are intelligently conservative, hard-working, and worthy because you got more than you said you were shooting for. A victory party celebrating an "over-the-top" campaign is festive, optimistic, full of smiling, satisfied faces. People love to associate with success and are drawn to it. Recruiting workers for a successful campaign is easier, certainly, than recruiting for a failure. Those who can take some of the credit, the committee, are surely going to serve again next year. The chairman takes on heroic stature. If professionals are involved, they look like wizards who, behind the scenes, guided the campaign to its triumph. Everybody wins. But how can that be? If everybody wins, who loses?

When you set your low goal, your inner group will automatically adjust their own gifts downward, in proportion to the goal. (For inner group members who don't want to give sacrificially, this could be another positive reason for the low goal.) And, as I've said several times already, when the inner group gives less, others give less. So a low goal could be costly unless the inner group maintains a relatively high giving level.

A low goal could set you back with foundations that don't want to give more than a certain percentage of the total to a campaign.

If you're raising money to buy a new ambulance for the hospital or to fix the roof on the church, it may not be important to have leather seats so long as you get the ambulance. And you can use a less expensive grade of roofing material so long as you fix the church roof. But suppose your low goal kept six additional kids from going to summer camp this year? Before I convince you that low goals are going to cheat a deserving child, remember you can't do everything! Low goals *can* be desirable and useful, particularly for untested campaigns.

THE HIGH GOAL. If you set your goal higher than you can reach, here's what *could* happen:

- By extending your reach beyond your grasp you may bring out the highest ideals of the members of your community and the hidden nobility in them.

- Your inner group members may give more than they had originally intended, adjusting to a higher goal.

- Prospects may adjust their sights too, and give in proportion to your goal.

- Your committee members may become inspired to reach heights they had never before imagined.

Here's what else could happen:

- You could be ridiculed because you can't justify the goal.

- You could fail miserably and nobody would want to associate with your project.

- You could inspire nobody.

- You could frighten your inner group members so badly they won't do anything for you.

THE ACTUAL GOAL. At first glance, you might think actual goals are best. They're honest, realistic, achievable, fair, true to your cause, and reflect an intelligent appraisal of the facts. But an actual goal that is barely reached could rob your group of the additional sense of satisfaction they get from going "over the top." Don't minimize the feeling—if you've had it you know what I mean. If you haven't I can tell you it's an exhilarating, heady sensation.

An actual goal lacks audacity. It diminishes inspiration and reduces the chances that your inner group will do the unexpected. And if a reserve fund isn't included in your goal, it leaves you vulnerable.

A low or actual goal could reduce the value of a windfall. Here's how: If someone makes an unexpected major gift or bequest that brings you to your goal or puts you over the top, your committee and chairman and prospects could decide there's no further reason to go on, or they may relax, slow down, and coast into the victory party.

NO GOAL. If you run a campaign with no goal, you eliminate the risk of failure. Whatever you raise is your goal. No goal may be the answer if you are out for the first time with no realistic list of donors, a modest inner group, or an obscure cause. A windfall can't finish your campaign; it will probably generate more money just as it would in a high-goal campaign. But in a no-goal campaign I won't know if my gift is 10 percent of what you need or .0001 percent. Should I give you fifty cents or fifty dollars? Will my gift make a dent in your project's budget?

As a committee member, where's my sense of accomplishment and satisfaction—do I feel it at $15,000 or $50,000 or $5 million? When do we finish the campaign, by the dollar or the calendar? How long will I have to be committed to the campaign?

I hope I have confused you about goals. It was intentional. I want you to give them the careful thought they deserve because there are no rules in setting goals—every campaign is different and may differ even from year to year. *You* have to decide what goals to set. All I can give you are the options, some guidelines, and a few pieces of advice.

Never establish a goal simply on the basis of need. Although your project is vitally important, it doesn't necessarily follow you are bound to fund it. I hope this is elementary to you because it wasn't to any number of people who have come to see me for advice. Have you ever followed up on one of those six o'clock TV news interviews where somebody says it will take $16,000 to buy a bus for the camp? Or an unspecified amount to do something else, and the person being interviewed is confident the "community" will respond? I have. The simple truth is they usually fail, leaving hurt, disillusioned people who were merely trying to do something worthwhile without thinking it through.

All right, then, what should a goal be based upon besides faith and good intentions?

The ten largest gifts to your campaign will usually total from one-third to one-half of the amount of money you can raise. *Not always,* usually. So if you are pretty sure you will get $20,000 from your top group, you can guess that with lots of hard work you will raise $40,000 to $60,000.

Don't stop there, however. If you've done a feasibility study, what did it bring out? Are there hidden sources of funds you haven't figured on? Or is the social climate turning against your project? (In the late sixties many college donors were turned off by campus unrest.) If you had a campaign last year, how much more, or less, do you think you can get from the same givers? Review your prospect ratings.* Be brutally honest—how much do you really think you'll get from them? Are the leaders of your campaign capable of turning up unexpected money? How much? Are they nice but weak?

Once you have arrived at a careful estimate of how much you think you can raise, you are ready to decide on a low, high, actual, or no goal. You'll know better than I whether to make people stretch or not. Whether they need the feeling of success, the challenge of an almost impossible task, or the safety of no goal. Your instincts will be right most of the time; trust them.

Table II (below) shows the size and the number of gifts you'll need for a $500,000 capital campaign—a building, endowment, or one-time project where contributors can pay their pledges over a period of three years. If your campaign is smaller or larger, just chop off or add some

*See Chapter 6 for ratings.

TABLE II
GIFTS NEEDED FOR A $500,000
CAPITAL FUND CAMPAIGN

Gift Size	Gifts Needed	Total
$50,000	1	$ 50,000
35,000	2	70,000
25,000	3	75,000
15,000	4	60,000
10,000	5	50,000
5,000	9	45,000
2,500	16	40,000
1,000	60	60,000
Under 1,000	Many	50,000
	100 +	$500,000

zeros after the dollar signs. Everything else stays the same, including the fact that your lead gift, your pace-setting gift, should always be at least 10 percent of your goal.

Notice in Table II that the ten biggest gifts are about half the goal and that 100 gifts total 90 percent of the goal. And finally, that the *many* represent only 10 percent of the total. I wasn't being undemocratic because in our democracy everybody does not have equal amounts of money. It's important to remember that 10 percent of the people have 90 percent of the money and the rest of us have the other 10 percent of the money. So, it's only logical that the rich be asked to give more because they have more.

Now then, how much should the campaign cost? I don't know and neither does anybody else. But here's a rule of thumb I use: If the campaign fails, it doesn't matter how much money you saved; if the campaign succeeds, it doesn't matter how much you spent, *within reason.*

I still haven't told you anything—you're looking for a

number with a percent sign. It doesn't work that way. It could cost you as much money, time, energy, heartache, and postage to raise $100,000 for one project as it would to raise $1 million for another. So a $20,000 cost could be 20 percent or 2 percent.

Fund raising shouldn't cost as much as running a business for profit because most of the work is done by volunteers and your contributor expects nothing in return but a receipt. But it will cost.

Will you need an office, a paid secretary, publicity people? How about an attorney and an accountant? Will you be planning luncheons, dinners, events? Are you thinking about hiring professional fund raising counsel? How about printing and postage and telephone and typewriters and paper clips?

Work with an accountant and tell him everything you are planning to do, everything you think you'll need, all the people you will have to hire, including messenger services and taxicabs. When he brings back a cost breakdown, add about 20 percent to the budget for the unexpected and underestimated. Then, if you can get another 10 percent of your costs free, you will have a reasonably accurate budget.

In budgeting, be prudent but not foolish. More campaigns fail because too little was spent on them, not too much. Spend where it will be valuable—hire the extra secretary if you need one, but forgo the fancy gifts to the committee.

Some local governments have ordinances that allow you to spend only a certain percentage of what you raise. Find out what they are—you may have to change some of your plans.

A final word on costs and budget. Don't start your campaign without enough money, *in advance,* to pay for it. If you're thinking you'll meet your obligations with money you raise as you go along, forget it. Your campaign will sputter and gasp like a Model T running out of gas. Just as your campaign is ready to have its kickoff dinner you won't have enough money to pay for the printing and postage of your invitations. Or you won't have enough money to fly to New York to talk to the Ford Foundation.

The Bureau of Labor Statistics will tell you most business bankruptcies happen because the business started without enough capital. The same is true for nonprofit organizations.

5

Constituencies, Lists, and Direct Mail

The dictionary I use defines "constituency" as "any body of supporters, customers, etc.; a clientele." The definition fits fund raising too.

Starting a fund raising campaign without a solid list of prospects is like setting up a pizza parlor on the Gobi Desert. You may have a wonderful product, but who's going to buy it? Some campaigns don't have to worry about finding their prospects—their constituency. They're built in—the members of the church, the alumni of the school, the patients, doctors, and community served by the hospital. But many campaigns don't have the luxury of a ready-made list of prospects. A public-interest project such as a halfway house for ex-convicts, a college with a small or poor alumni group, a project in a poor neighborhood may all deserve support, but the question is, who will give it?

Nonconstituency fund raising is not only hard to pronounce, it's the toughest kind of campaign. But there are things you *can* do to build a good prospect list from scratch.

TIMELINESS. In October 1957 the Russians launched Sputnik. Immediately the call went out for engineers, physicists, and a vast group of scientists to prepare a comparable U.S. space program. It was a bonanza for colleges and universities. Alumni, foundation, and government funds poured in for laboratories, equipment, scholarships, and faculty.

How timely is your project? Is there some aspect of it that can capture the attention of prospects whose interest span is directly related to today's newspaper headlines? If there is, take advantage of it; there's nothing wrong in being opportunistic. I don't suggest you distort your project to fit the headlines. I do suggest you do what many hospitals did when the drug problem was on every TV newscast and front page: they called attention to their own drug-abuse programs, even though many were small and understaffed. As a result, many prospects practically identified themselves.

LOGIC. Every parent, grandparent, relative, and friend of an afflicted child is an obvious logical prospect for your leukemia research project. There are other logical but *not so obvious* constituents out there. Is there a service club— Kiwanis, Lions, Knights of Pythias—that might take your campaign under its wing and supply manpower and prospects? What about the Auto Wreckers' Association as a prospect for your ecology or safety campaign? How about Mensa* and your retarded children's home? There is something about your campaign that is unique. Find it and find the group or individuals that dovetail into it.

BRAINSTORMING. This is the best way to build your prospect list. Sit down in a quiet place with a pencil and a large pad of paper. Write down the names of everyone you know. Everyone! Don't leave anybody out; you can

---

*Mensa is a national organization made up of people with a score on an intelligence test higher than that of 98 percent of the general population.

always cut the list later. Include your auto mechanic, your lawyer, your boss's secretary, everybody you do business with, the places where you have clout. Soon you will find the names on your list will suggest other names you had forgotten about. Uncle Max! He moved to Alaska years ago and the last you heard he was doing very well. The guy you met on the plane who talked about something similar to your project. I once brainstormed with the president of a small, poor college. After three hours, we had a list of people that astonished him. People we could talk to, send presentations to, and solicit with a reasonable chance for success. Your list, if you do it right, will astonish you too. Take your time. Let the names bubble to the surface as they surely will.

Then get everybody in your inner group to do the same thing. Explain to them how to do it, and help them. When they finish their lists, bring them all together to brainstorm as a group. The same results will emerge and you will have a list of prospects where none existed before.

Even though they may not be part of your inner group, every contributor becomes a potential brainstormer. Ask them for their help—the worst they can do is say no.

RESEARCH.   Almost all nonprofit groups put their trustees and advisory councils on their letterheads. Check out the names on those letterheads if the group has some bearing on your project. Add those names to your list only if someone in your inner family has a contact with them.

Foundations have board members too. Check out their names with your inner group. If someone involved in your project has a close relationship with a foundation board member, it could start you on a foundation strategy you couldn't have put together any other way.

Review the names of every elected official in your area. The local library will probably have the names of staff members of officials and political appointees. If you know a member of the Athletic Commission, would he introduce you to the owner of the local professional football team?

If you don't know about it already, it could surprise you how much you can find out about people without trying; particularly about rich people, famous people, top executives, and socially prominent people.

Just for the fun of it I looked up a corporate executive I know, in only three sources, and here's what I found: From *Poor's Register of Corporations, Directors and Executives,* his birth year and place; the schools he went to and the years he graduated; the name and address of the company he works for; his title in the company; his home address; the names of other companies where he's a board member; the name of a college where he's a trustee; the names of the other officers in the company he works for and their titles; what his company does, how many employees it has, and the dollar volume of their business; the names of the companies in the same industry. From the *Social Register* I found his unlisted home phone number and his wife's maiden name. From *Who's Who in America* I found his father's name and his mother's maiden name; his college degrees; his wedding date; the names of his children; awards he received and who bestowed them; and the social clubs he belongs to.

Your librarian can lead you to other printed sources if you want and need more information. If my corporate friend was a member of your inner group, here's what you could do: You could add to your list all the names of other executives in his companies, and the names of the corporations on whose boards he sits and their executives. You add them not necessarily as prospects, but as suspects. They become prospects when the executive says he'll ask them for a contribution.

Everything I've told you about timeliness, logic, brainstorming, and research goes double if you already have a constituency. Broaden your prospect base by talking to the doctors in your hospital's project. Have they reviewed their files of former patients? It's perfectly ethical. That rich former patient may not know the hospital needs money for an important research program and might be anxious to help. What about the law firm of your church member or alumnus? The process of building your prospect list should be continuous. People die, move, or lose interest, and unless you are constantly adding names, your list will shrink.

When you sift through your list, please take out the names of the Tisch Brothers. Sure they have lots of money—so does the Rockefeller family. Do you have an even remote point of contact with them? I know you won't be guilty of such foolishness, but you would be amazed at how many people are. They don't put down Rockefeller's name, but they do include the name of everybody they can think of who is rich, whether or not he might be remotely interested in the project or whether or not anyone in the inner group could contact him.

Clean your list regularly—check it for new addresses and remove the names of those who are gone. Be sure you spell people's names right! And don't send a Mr. and Mrs. note to a recent widow. List maintenance is a big job if you have a big list. Somebody should be in charge of it, working at it all the time.

When you have a reasonably good list—at least a thousand live prospects or givers—you have another avenue open to you for building your constituency. It's called list swapping.

There are list-maintenance companies, list-compiling companies, list brokers, and other organizations like yours eager to know the names on your list. So you swap lists— for every thousand names you give them you get a thousand names. When it's done right it's not bad provided the list you're getting is one you want, people who could have some interest in your project. Don't get a list of motorcycle owners for your philosophical think tank. There's another catch: if it's done right you won't be able to review the names on *their* list because you won't see their list and they won't see yours. They'll send you one thousand envelopes, letters, and whatever else they want their people to get, and you address the envelopes with your names and mail them out. They do the same thing for you.

You could rent out your list if it gets big enough. Prices range from $20 to $60 per thousand names and up and you can rent out a good list often. But that's up to you. Isn't that sneaky and immoral? No. Like you, I get dozens of letters every month trying to sell me something or asking me for money. My name must be on a thousand lists. Some of the junk mail I just throw away, but like you, every once in a while I read a letter that moves me. I learn about something I didn't know before and I respond. I suppose if anybody should complain, it's the mailman—he has to carry the letters I don't open.

From list brokers to direct-mail fund raising is a logical sequence—you almost have to have the one if you want to do the other. Direct mail is used by many national organizations to find hidden donors. Fund raising by mail has certain advantages: the work is done mostly by machines, you don't have to look a contributor in the eye, and the mailman delivers the money.

However, direct mail today normally costs about two dollars for every new dollar raised. The gross profit comes from renewals (people who gave last year and will give again this year when you send them another letter). But even renewals have a high ratio of cost to income, and may take years to develop.

Let me give you an example. A Washington, D.C.-based

environmental group began a direct-mail campaign some years ago. After seven years of mail activity, they were raising more than $500,000 per year. But, their costs were still 40 percent of the amount they raised. I do not know whether there was any other way they could have raised as much money, and I certainly do not accuse them of being crooked. What I am saying is direct mail can be an expensive method of raising money.

Direct mail does build a contributors' list fast and you could find a nugget or two when the envelopes come in. If you have a large staff of volunteers or professionals, you can research every contributor and you may come up with a few millionaires to solicit personally for a large gift.

Via direct mail you can reach thousands of potential givers you could never reach any other way. One small national health agency raises $3 million every year through the mail. With a highly efficient, sophisticated computer system that does everything including envelope licking, they have reduced their costs to $1 million per year.

If you finally decide to try direct mail for your project, please don't do it by yourself unless one of your inner group is an expert. Hire a professional, but fire him on the spot if he doesn't suggest a test mailing first. Then be careful or he may load the test with a list of proven givers (those lists do exist but the number of names is limited) and you'll get a response much greater than you would with a random list, and your test would be unrealistic. Check the professional's past clients. Talk to them at length. They'll be happy to help a struggling group like yours.

As of this writing, your mail test should cost between 50 and 75 cents a letter—probably more—plus the cost of list rental. If you use color, fancy brochures and envelopes, costs will skyrocket. A test of 25,000 for a national mailing should be big enough. But test 5,000 names from 5 different lists if you want a fair test. With luck this is what will happen: 25,000 letters at 50 cents a letter = $12,500; 25,000 names rented at $40 per thousand = $1,000. Total cost: $13,500. A 1 percent response (above average for typical direct mail) from 25,000 letters = 250 returns. If there's an average of $25 in each returned envelope, that's $6,250, or below half what you spent.

You should make up the losses in the following years as you ask your contributors to give again, as shown in Table III.

You noticed, I hope, that I didn't figure costs of the people who are doing all the work. And, I figured postage at the current pre-cancelled bulk rate for nonprofit organizations, not first class mail. Neither did I add in the cost of hiring a direct mail professional.

I would recommend direct-mail fund raising to you if you're sure nothing else will work, or if you already have adequate funding sources and just want to build a list of moderate givers over a wide geographical area.

Remember there is a danger that you might get a small gift from a potentially big contributor if you use direct mail. Remember too, direct mail will not produce instant money—it will take time before you raise much more than you spend.

Is there an art to direct-mail fund raising? Well, yes and no. Choosing the right lists takes experience. It's not enough to know the easy ones (that a list of auto dealers in Arizona may not draw a response for your Maine wildlife project). There are subtleties that require knowledge of lists, where to get them, how to swap, when to go back to one that worked before. It takes experience to know when the letters ought to be mailed, how many times to send a prospect a letter, and when. Getting the right

TABLE III
TYPICAL PATTERN OF DIRECT MAIL
GIVING AND RENEWED GIVING*

Year	% Of Last Year's Donors Who Will Probably Repeat	Number of Donors	Average Gift	Amount Raised	Cost of Raising it
1990	—	250	$25	$ 6,250	$13,500
1991	60%	150	25	3,750	125
1992	80%	120	25	3,000	75
1993	80%	96	25	2,400	60
1994	80%	77	25	1,925	48
1995	80%	62	25	1,550	38.50
			TOTALS	$17,875	$13,846.50

*Table III is based upon our example of 25,000 pieces of mail sent in 1990 at a cost of $13,500, with a 1 percent return—250 gifts—and an average of $25 per gift. The 1991 cost is based upon sending letters only to the 250 donors from 1990 at 50 cents each, and so on.

person to sign the letter can make a big difference. It takes experience to know who that person might be and how to get him to agree.

The art in direct mail is in the letter itself. What it says, how it says it; the use of language to make an idea come alive and compel you to write a check.

So if you feel your project has a national constituency waiting to hear from you, you may want to try direct mail. Try it with care, know what your chances are, but avoid it if you have *any* other way to raise money.

Here is a sample letter (I made up the project). I don't claim it would bring in a flood of contributions—letters rarely do. But it makes its case using easy-to-understand language, it's brief, personal, and human, and it asks for a direct gift of a specific amount.

THE FOUNDATION FOR RESEARCH
IN THE CAUSES OF AGING

July 9

Mr. Caldwell Cadwallader
123 Bohemian Street
New Orleans, Louisiana 70113

Dear Mr. Cadwallader:

Nobody really understands why people grow old or how. If we're unlucky and something kills us before old age sets in, we may not be that unlucky after all. In most cases what we have to look forward to can be a bleak existence, possible senility, or a lingering death.

Sounds pretty horrible, doesn't it?

Somehow we manage to spend millions on the problems of the young and we should, they're *our* children and our hope for the future, but isn't it ironic that we ignore ourselves as we grow older?

The Foundation for Research in the Causes of Aging is looking for some answers to very hard questions. We're not fooling ourselves and we don't want to fool you into thinking we are just around the corner from a breakthrough. We're not. But there aren't too many places where our kind of research is going on.

We need your help. For example, one of our small computers costs $38 a day to operate. Would you help keep it running for a day or two?

You have probably seen that wonderful picture of two smiling, elderly, gray-haired people walking arm in arm into the sunset. We're trying to make it come true for everybody.

P.S. The enclosed booklet has more information about us.

6

Ratings, Assignments, and Reports

In his book *Democracy in America,* Alexis de Tocqueville wrote:

These Americans are the most peculiar people in the world. You'll not believe me when I tell you how they behave. In a local community in their country a citizen may conceive of some need which is not being met. What does he do? He goes across the street and discusses it with his neighbor. Then what happens? A committee comes into existence and the committee begins functioning in behalf of that need.

De Tocqueville wrote that more than 150 years ago. With uncanny accuracy he predicted what you are doing right now. You have a committee, a chairman, and a goal, and your case is spelled out clearly. De Tocqueville didn't say what the next step would be, but I will.

You call a meeting of your committee and plan your campaign. Your meeting should determine:

1. Your potential givers.
2. How much each should give.
3. Who will ask whom.
4. When.

Let's assume you have a good list of potential givers for your campaign. How much will they give? As I've said, rarely more than the largest gift of a member of your inner group. Keeping that in mind—and throw it out if it doesn't fit your condition—go over your list of prospects to figure out what would be a reasonable gift for each one. These are some things you should consider when rating prospects: How rich are they? How close are they to your project? How much do they give to other worthy causes? How high on their priority list would your project be? Do you have members of your committee who can influence the prospects? The right person asking the right person can get significantly more money than the wrong person doing the asking.

This process of rating prospects is very important. It will help you to determine your campaign goal; it will give your askers information they must have before they can ask; it shows the prospect you have given careful thought to your campaign; it lets him know what you are thinking about—whether you are asking for $10, $100, $10,000.

When you are satisfied with your ratings, you are ready to assign each prospect to a member of your committee. Here are some do's:

1. Assign your best prospects to your most influential askers.

2. Set a limit on the number of assignments to each committee member. Try to keep that number under a dozen.

3. Try to get two or more committee members to work as teams on top prospects.

4. Set a date when your committee will meet again to discuss results, usually no more than two weeks away.

5. Be sure your committee members know the answers to any possible questions about your project.

6. Call your committee members within three days to remind them of their assignments.

7. Keep accurate records of who is supposed to see whom.

8. Try to give everyone at least one assignment that will result in a contribution.

9. Make sure every committee member has made a sacrificial gift in advance.

Some don'ts:

1. Don't assign a $1,000 prospect to a committee member who is giving $100.

2. Don't assign a prospect simply because an eager committee member wants it. Giver and asker should fit!

3. Don't allow your committee members to contact their prospects by letter unless the prospect lives too far away to be seen in person.

Now that your prospects are assigned, you may want to plan an event to give your committee and prospects a focus for giving and asking. If not, your committee can begin its work immediately. Tomorrow. But no later.

Now send your committee members out to do their jobs. This is a critical time for your campaign because campaigns fail more often for lack of askers, rather than lack of prospects. Committee members, as askers, put things off, or don't know what to say or how to say it.

Asking for a contribution is really very easy if you remember a few, simple rules, some of which you already know:

1. Know as much about your project as possible.

2. Make your own gift first, and make it sacrificial.

3. Know your prospect. Figure out the best conditions possible for asking for the gift.

4. See the prospect in person.

5. Tell your prospect how much you are giving and ask

for the amount you hope he'll give. This is the hardest part. You think it's rude and uncouth. Actually, you are doing him a favor and here's why: By telling how much you are giving you have let him know how important the project is to you and that you are prepared to put your money on the line for it. And, by asking for a definite amount—you can say something like, "Would you consider a gift in the range of $200?"—you have relieved him of a possible embarrassment. If you don't specify, he might not know what to do—whether $200 would make him look like a cheapskate or a show-off. He can still say no to the $200 question, but at least you both know what he said no to. There's always the chance, on the other hand, that he'll be flattered at your high opinion of him.

6. Once you've asked for the contribution, keep quiet! Don't say another word. Really! If there's a secret to asking for money for a charitable cause, this is it. You will be tempted to break the silence that follows your $200 question. Don't. Wait for your prospect to think about it and mull it over. The longer it takes for an answer, the greater the tension and *you* want *him* to break the tension with a pledge. If you're patient, he probably will.

That's all there is to it, so don't let anybody tell you that asking for money is a mysterious ritual known only to a few of the people on the inside. Some will try to sell you the formula and they'll throw in 500 shares of the New York subway system for an extra few bucks.

At the report meeting two weeks away, your committee members can share experiences—tell each other which approach worked and which didn't. Let them bask in their successes and sympathize with each other over their failures. The report meeting is a time to assign prospects left over from the last meeting. Give those assignments to committee members who have done well on their first batch. If any of your top prospects were talked to unsuccessfully, discuss ways of going back to them. Maybe a new asker or a new approach might work. Top gift prospects are hard to replace, so don't give up on them after one failure.

The process of report meetings, new assignments, and reassignment of prospects can go on for many weeks. But you must have a date on which you finish your campaign. That date depends upon how many prospects you have and how many askers you have. If you're in a $150 million campaign for Dartmouth College, the professional staff will be there to guide you every step along the way. But if your objective is, say $80,000 for a local summer camp and you're working without professional help, the campaign should not take more than about four weeks from your first committee meeting to your victory celebration. Take as much time as you need *to get ready* for the campaign, but don't expect your committee to stay dedicated for more than a month or so.

While your campaign is in progress keep in touch with the committee regularly. If the size of your group warrants it, prepare a weekly newsletter and get everybody's name in it. Show how the campaign is going—how much is in and how much is yet to go. Keep it light and upbeat—don't be gloomy or push panic buttons.

When you schedule your first committee meeting, also schedule a party of some kind for the last day of the campaign. You could invite your contributors, and the party might even be a setting where you recruit a contributor or two for your inner group. Give out awards in recognition of what people did that made your campaign a success. Have one of the kids from the summer camp present, or a model of the new wing on the hospital.

All this is fine, you say, but it doesn't apply in your case because:

1. We have a very small inner group.
2. We're brand-new and can't rate our prospects.
3. We have a vague list of prospects.
4. We'll settle for small contributions because our goal is small.
5. Our inner group is dedicated but really poor.

Then you will probably have to schedule a special event. (See Chapter 10 for more information about special events.) Be sure you pick an event best suited to your special case. You do that by the process of elimination. Rule out the obvious nonapplicable events first—an opera group might plan a gourmet dinner but you shouldn't plan one to raise money for starving kids. You wouldn't plan a gambling junket to Las Vegas on behalf of the Salvation Army. Nor should you plan to sell ten thousand $5 tickets to an event if you have only ten committee members. Above all, rule out any event that depends solely upon publicity for success.

For special events the timetable changes. Preparation will take longer and so will the campaign itself. There is an easy way to figure out a timetable for fund raising, whether it's a special event or the traditional campaign of assignments and follow-up. Work backward.

Figure out the date of your event or victory party. Then put down on paper a calendar running backward from that date listing the time for report meetings, publicity releases, printing, mailing, contacting people, and everything else that applies to your case listed on the special-event checklist in the Appendix.

Give yourself enough time to do it right and stick to your schedule!

★ ★ ★

You've given it your best but your campaign failed—what do you do now?

Don't sit around and moan about your fate or accuse the community of being near-sighted. The failure was yours, not theirs.

As soon as you can, call your inner group together for a long session. Get them before they abandon the project. You won't have to come up with an imaginative excuse for the meeting. Just tell them to come because they are needed now more than ever.

The meeting should not be structured—no formal agenda, just a bull session. Give your group a chance to get things off their chests; a gripe that comes up for air doesn't fester. Everybody should get a chance to voice opinions and complaints. When the air has cleared a bit, pose these questions, openly, honestly, to find out what really went wrong and what you might do to salvage your project:

1. Did you run your campaign at the wrong time? Was the social climate against you? Were you raising scholarship money for a college that was in the middle of a student unrest problem? Was your group under fire by the mass communications media, by the community, or by your own constituents? Was an older, better organized group working in the same general field reaching your constituents one step ahead of you?

2. Did people really understand your project? Did your committee really understand everything there was to know about your project?

3. Did you have a list of prospects that was logical, people with a known relationship to your project or its leaders? Did you take the time to rate each project carefully? Were the prospects assigned with equal care? Were the prospects seen in person by a reliable committee member or team?

4. Did your inner group make truly sacrificial gifts? Did

any committee member solicit a gift without telling the prospect how much he, the solicitor, gave first?

5. When you added up your inner-group pledges and the ratings of your prospects, were you woefully short of the money you needed? Did you go ahead on pure faith?

6. Did you rely too heavily on publicity? Was the letter your primary fund raising tool? Did you think your printed brochure was the campaign.

7. Was your leadership weak? Was there dissension about who would do what and who would get the credit? Did your leaders follow up every possibility? Did they let the campaign drag on and on without any definite plan? Were your leaders more concerned about the trappings and prestige of leadership than the responsibility.

Somewhere in the seven categories is the reason for your failure. If you can find it and correct it, you may still be able to salvage your campaign. It won't be easy—it may even be impossible—but if you're willing to try, here are some more suggestions:

Give yourself one more week. Not two, one! See how much of the money you still need can be made up by the inner group—right now at the meeting! Ask them for it! Review the ratings and gifts of your top prospects only. Did they give as much as they could have? Devise a new strategy for each one, carefully, and maybe you can get them to increase.

I must warn you there is nothing harder in fund raising than a warmed-over campaign. The only bright note I have is that if you follow the sequences for your campaign that I have outlined, you probably won't have to go back and do it over again.

7

Why People Give

Out there somewhere, hiding behind drawn curtains, guarding his checkbook with the zeal of a latter-day Scrooge, lurks the prospect. His secretary has orders to deny entry to anyone with the slightest aroma of solicitor on him. He is a combination of the Artful Dodger, Sneaky Pete, Speedy Gonzales, and Judge Crater. He is by turns whimsical, stubborn, capricious, Victorian, invisible, rebellious, and downright ignorant. And all you have to do is convert him into a true believer, a giver.

I'm exaggerating, you say. Well, I've watched people review a list of potential givers as though they were getting ready for a battle against a well-armed enemy. They referred to prospects in language that would send an Army sergeant dashing for the dictionary. At other times they treated the campaign as though it were a battle of wits—a duel with "them."

Some years ago the great cartoonist Walt Kelly, creator of Pogo, had his animal characters preparing themselves for a possible invasion. Scouts were sent out, and when they returned one of them said, "We have met the enemy and he is us."

He *is* us and he's a friend, not an enemy.

He's pitched, solicited, importuned, pressured, cajoled,

and bombarded. But he gives. There are times when he would like to hide; he rarely does. There are times when he'd like to call a halt to all the appeal he gets. They seem to come at him from a thousand sources and each has a thousand reasons for him to contribute and he wishes they would go away. But he gives.

And he gives for many different reasons. You can probably add another dozen to the ten I picked as my list: Love. Hate. Fear. Shame. Guilt. Friendship. Loyalty. Nostalgia. To impress others. To impress himself.

But the most important reason he'll give is that *somebody asked him*. (Yes, back to that again.)

Does that mean the cause isn't important? Of course not. But spontaneous, unsolicited, significant contributions are rarer than empty taxicabs in a rainstorm.

Think about yourself for a minute: When was the last time *you* sent a check to a cause without being asked? Does that make you a cheapskate?

But suppose your boss or your neighbor asked you to buy $10 worth of tickets to the Frarmish School annual picnic and fish fry; could you turn him down?

The best way to learn about prospective givers is to think about yourself, because *you're* a prospect for somebody else's campaign. Are you stupid, insensitive, oblivious of the world around you? Do you laugh when you hear about somebody's misfortune? Would you turn your back on a helpless child?

You can't give to everything and neither can people much richer than you. A $10 giver has to give as much thought to his gift as a $10,000 giver. Both have to establish priorities. Almost nobody has enough money to respond to every cause that sends him a letter, or puts on a telethon, or advertises in the papers and magazines.

So what do you do? Chances are you do what everybody else does—when you give, you give because you were asked. I don't mean to suggest that you or anybody else always gives when asked. Of course you turn down many requests, but let me repeat, when you *do* give, somebody asked you. And your campaign will succeed or fail depending upon the number of people who ask and the number of people who are asked.

If you think about it, you'll be surprised at how many ways you can be asked to give money to a good cause. I mentioned the telethon, the letter, and the newspaper or magazine ad. Then there's the telephone, the billboard, the counter-top coin box, the TV and radio spot announcements, the door-to-door collection, the message from the pulpit, the raffle, the charity auction, the umpteen-dollar-a-plate dinner, the concert, the bake sale, the flea market, and as many others as the ingenuity of clever minds can come up with. Which one gets the most money from *you*? Do you see the difference in appeal between an approach from a real live person as opposed to a coin box, for example?

Okay. I've made my point. You as giver respond best when somebody looks you in the eye and asks. Now, what gets the most from you? How do you set your giving priorities?

A child falls into an abandoned mine shaft and within hours TV and radio crews are on the spot. Volunteers pour in from all over and elected officials appear like mushrooms after a rain. Spontaneous fund raising begins with checks and cash from local citizens, TV viewers, volunteers, and officials. We set up a national vigil and we interrupt everything for the hourly report from the scene of the action. When the child is rescued you can almost hear more than 200 million Americans shout, "Hurrah," with us among the shouters. At the same time thousands of Americans—many of them children—live in fear of death every day because we have a shortage of dialysis machines, artificial kidneys that take the place of kidneys no longer working properly.

Ask eight psychiatrists and you'll get ten theories why we react the way we do to the child in the mine shaft and the children with diseased kidneys. My choice is the one that says the child in the mine shaft is someone we can identify with. One child is small enough for us to understand and reach out our hand to.

A scale model of the new hospital is a pretty thing, with miniature trees and cars—a nice toy, and it gives people an idea of what the finished hospital will look like. But the hospital is a *thing* like a dialysis machine. While some people will respond to an appeal for a thing, many more will respond to a sick child, a crippled adult, a tired, frightened, lonely older person. Wouldn't you?

When you think about the potential giver, try to think how you can make your project personal for him. A library is not just a building with books in it. It's a place where young minds learn to grow, where people get information that makes them better neighbors and citizens. Research on cancer is not just machines and test tubes in a laboratory, it's the possible cure for a human being ravaged by a horrible disease. A college is people, Boy Scouts are people, restoring the shoreline of Lake Michigan is for people.

And your project, whatever it is, is for people, too. It shouldn't take you long to translate your campaign into human terms, and once you've done it, stay with it.

I have attended many seminars where psychologists have talked about dozens of reasons people give money away. They are always right—in their own way. They review the motivational forces at work that make people charitable. The psychologists can make giving sound terribly complicated, which it is. But they rarely go into the most important reason of all, *people give to people,* and if I have to say it five hundred times, I will, because that's the nub of fund raising.

Treat your prospective giver like a human being. Get to know him, if you can. Find out about his interests, his family, his business, his background, his school. Talk to his friends and his family. Get to know as much about him as good taste permits. Somewhere in the information you put together may be the clue you need to clinch his gift, or prevent you from saying something to turn him off.

Not long ago during a college campaign we found out that the wife of a wealthy alumnus had recently died. He had been figured as a good prospect for the campaign. We also learned that his late wife loved music and had given up a promising career to marry. With that information it was possible to persuade the alumnus to make a large contribution for a scholarship in music named for his wife.

Find out, if you can, who has influence on your prospective giver. Does he respect and listen to his minister, his business partner, his barber? If you can, enlist the help of the person with influence.

All I'm really telling you is: Do your homework!

Now what about the major givers, the special prospects who can make or break your campaign?

They know more about philanthropy and the relative value of different appeals and causes than most of us do. They have to because they're solicited constantly.

A few of my more cynical colleagues are sure philanthropy would vanish overnight if tax laws on charitable deductions were abolished. They're wrong. De Tocqueville was right—Americans will see something that needs to be done and they'll do it, with or without a tax break.

If your child had leukemia and you could afford to give $50,000 for leukemia research, would you be concerned about a tax deduction?

Of course rich people check with their accountants and lawyers on how much they can give away. While there aren't many tax shelters left, there are estate plans that can save donors and their families large sums of money. You would do what they do if you could. Those are the rules as they now stand, and everyone plays the Internal Revenue Service game every year.

Benjamin Harrison Swig, who owned the Fairmont Hotel in San Francisco, was one of America's great philanthropists. Every year he gave away, personally, more than many good-sized foundations. I once asked him why he did it—why he was so generous to so many causes.

"I enjoy it!" he said. "This country has been good to me and I want to give back as much as I can and I want to do it while I'm alive."

Then he added something that could be used, in part at least, as a philosophy for all of us. "I'm on the board of several foundations that were set up when some of my rich friends died. I'm having all the fun of giving *their* money away. They made the money, but I'm the one enjoying it. They were too busy, but I'm not too busy to give their money to colleges and hospitals and all the important things that need help."

While Ben Swig was a remarkable man, he was not singular; there are thousands of him all over the country and I've met many of them. Had I not met them, I'd know they were there anyway—120 billion philanthropic dollars didn't appear by magic in 1990.

So while the big prospect is not just sitting around hoping you'll call, he does exist, he's not an ogre, neither is he a fool. He's really you and me with lots more money.

8

Publicity

There is one mistake new organizations make most often (and some older ones too): they think publicity raises money.

Publicity *doesn't* raise money. It never did, and unless the American character takes on some new dimensions, it never will. The best it can do for you is help you create a favorable climate for your campaign. The worst it can do is make people think you have all the money you need because everybody knows about you.

There are four things the mass communications media can say about you and three will hurt: You're good, you're bad, you're controversial, not enough is known about you.

There is nothing deader than yesterday's newspaper, which is traditionally used to wrap fish. The radio or television exposure you get lasts a brief moment, and you're the only one listening anyway. Even when you get the radio or television station to run your message intact, including a post office box number for people to send money to, almost nobody listens. The ones who do listen forget the box number. The ones who remember don't respond and the ones who respond don't send enough to cover your costs.

A full-blown publicity campaign can be very expensive

unless it's confined to a small town. In big cities you almost have to hire a professional and give him an expense account. You'll probably need a photographer, messenger services, additional printing and photocopying, and all for what? The chance something about your project may show up on page 17 of the paper.

But every other campaign seems to get gobs of coverage; they must know what they're doing. Well, among my recent clients were four multimillion-dollar campaigns without a publicity program. We didn't need any. We had askers and givers, a strong case and a campaign plan.

The School of the Ozarks raises several million a year. If you've even heard of the School of the Ozarks you probably memorize Chesapeake and Ohio Railroad time-tables. (The School of the Ozarks is a fine eighty-seven-year-old private college in Point Lookout, Missouri, with about a thousand students.) They don't worry about publicity because they are obviously well organized.

Unless you have a human-interest story or there's something about your project that merits a feature article, you'll have to deal with the news people at the paper or TV station. And they want news, not puffery. You may want and need a story in the media in advance of the $100-a-plate dinner on your schedule. But it's not news in advance. The media may cover the dinner, and you'll get your publicity the next day after it's over. What good will that do you?

At the annual banquet of one of my clients, a famous movie producer suffered an apparent heart attack. The heart attack made headlines, our project didn't.

You have to figure out what publicity will do for you as a fund raising tool. Don't confuse your campaign with the urgency of a war, the appeal of the Olympics or a national election. Those are news stories, not the drumbeats of a charity drive.

Dependency on publicity is often the mark of an unorganized, lazy campaign. In most cases those who suggest mass publicity are people who don't want to do anything for their project. When their publicity campaign fails to make the cover of *Time*, they use it as an excuse for not working.

But before you start thinking I have a vendetta against publicity people or the media, relax. I don't. There are many campaigns that need media exposure.

You should consider publicity:

1. If you're like the Heart Fund, for example, with an army of people ready to ring every doorbell in your area. A saturation publicity campaign prepares the prospect so he recognizes the charity even though he may not know much more than the name. If you're having an event that depends on selling a lot of tickets to a lot of people and your committee is well organized in advance, publicity will help.

2. If your campaign is in the public interest but you have a relatively small prospect list. Publicity may educate enough people to enlarge your constituency. But you'd better have a plan ready to take advantage of your new friends. They won't come to you.

3. If you're in a small community. An item in the *Duncan* (Oklahoma) *Banner* (population 23,000) will be seen by almost everybody in town and would help the Boys' Club project. But an item in the *New York Times* about a Brooklyn Boys' Club is meaningless to a Manhattan reader. Besides, the item would be buried so deeply that even Brooklyn readers wouldn't find it.

4. If your inner group members need the flattery of seeing their names or pictures in the paper and it will make them work harder.

5. If a major donor will be kept happy and involved by reading about himself or seeing himself on television.

6. If your project is looking for money from government sources and your publicity shows you have thousands of supporters. It may influence the elected officials who see it.

7. If you're trying to overcome a negative public attitude toward your project. During periods of campus unrest, many schools launch massive publicity campaigns to combat the resistance of their donors.

8. If you're similar to the American Cancer Society or the United Way, you're going to be around year after year after year—and you need to remind people constantly about your good work.

9. If you're more than halfway through your campaign and the rest is in the bag. At that point you can *announce* your campaign. It could act as a spur to your committee members so they'll finish their job.

10. If you're in a public-interest project like prison reform or conservation and you want to arouse public sentiment. But don't expect money to pour in because there was a news story about you. You're still going to have to organize a fund raising campaign.

If you fit one of the ten categories or you want a publicity program in spite of everything I've said, my best advice is to hire a professional. If you can't or won't, then try to act like one yourself. The public library is chock-full of good books about the subject and you ought to read at least one.

You should know the difference between a news story and a promotion piece, and stick to news. You should know the deadlines of each outlet to which you're going to send material. You should know how to write a news release. You should time your publicity campaign to coincide with your fund raising. You should know the names of the people in the media outlets and address your material to them.

If you have a legitimate, important news story, know how to schedule a press conference and the kinds of materials you'll need there. You should know the audience you're trying to reach and which media outlet will reach them. You should know what a real feature story is, how to write it, and where you might be able to place it. A feature story is something interesting but not necessarily timely. A story about a staff doctor at your hospital and how he overcame polio to become an expert in childhood diseases is a feature. If he's going to operate on the governor's son, that's news.

Don't get mad at the media for not using your material. They don't owe you anything. Don't use pressure to get your material in print or on the air. It may work, but only once.

Obviously I haven't scratched the surface of the things you need to know to run a good publicity campaign. So I'll repeat, hire a professional. Don't try to recruit one for your committee because you think he might work for nothing. He'll probably resent it or be working for a paying client when you need him most, or both.

We get a staggering number of sales messages every day from papers, radio, television, the mail, billboards, neon signs, the phone—even drive-in movies have commercials.

If you think your publicity campaign can compete with those messages, fine. When you add the demands of business, family pressures, and the incessant hammering of news stories about the economy, energy, domestic crisis after crisis, foreign crisis after crisis—the average American should be cringing in a corner someplace. It's a tribute to his sanity and durability that he hasn't cracked yet.

Do you still think your publicity campaign is going to get through to him and persuade him? Really?

9

Lessons I Have Learned

Earlier I talked about some chickens I have dropped in more than thirty years as a professional. It wasn't a casual statement to make you feel good—I *have* made some mistakes, and I learned something from each one.

I'm going to tell you about some of them and the lessons they taught me. You might as well take advantage of my experiences, because I have.

★   ★   ★

The Incident. I'm sure you're familiar with invocations—someone asks for the blessings of God before a group gets on with its regular business. This invocation was delivered at a fund raising dinner in Montreal. It was the major event for a church-building fund, and we had invited a popular local clergyman to deliver the invocation before we sat down to eat. The chairman introduced the clergyman and asked him to come to the microphone just as forty waiters came out of the kitchen carrying huge trays of food. Out of respect, the waiters stood silently with their trays as the invocation was read. But it turned out not to be a simple, brief blessing. After five minutes of invocation, the waiters couldn't hold their trays overhead so they put them on the tables. The audience, sitting with bowed heads, began to look around, confused. After fifteen minutes the waiters sat down on the floor and the audience became restless. After thirty minutes the waiters stretched out on the floor and the famished audience began snatching food from the trays. Their mood could be described as surly. By the time our clergyman was finished, the dining room was a shambles. He had delivered a full-blown oratorical masterpiece that lasted more than an hour. We learned later he thought he was the major speaker and felt it was curious he was asked to speak before dinner. We didn't raise a dime.

LESSON. Always have a typewritten agenda for *any* meeting you schedule. The agenda should show the exact sequence of speakers and how much time each has been allotted. It should show the precise order of business, which comes first, who does what and when. Everyone who has a speaking role at a meeting must be talked to in advance. Find out what they're going to say so they don't duplicate one another. Tell them how much time they are allowed and try to get copies of their speeches so you can check them. The average speaker talks at the rate of about 150 words per minute, so count the words in the speech. Leave nothing to chance.

★ ★ ★

The Incident. While working on a national health campaign some years ago I talked to a world-famous entertainer about performing at a $100-a-plate dinner in Denver, Colorado. He was gracious and interested and agreed to do it free. The day before the event he called me to confirm all the arrangements—his airplane flight number, rehearsal piano player, hotel suite, limousine at the Denver airport, everything. When his flight arrived at Denver, a committee made up of local dignitaries and campaign leaders was waiting. So were reporters, photographers, radio and television crews. Our star never got off the plane because he hadn't gotten on it in the first place. He just didn't bother to show up or let anybody know about it.

LESSON. Most famous personalities, entertainers, and movie stars are as dependable as Big Ben. They will do what they say they will do. But they usually live and work under impossible schedules with great pressures and demands upon their time and talent. Always understand your star attraction might *cancel* an appearance for a hundred different reasons and you'll be left high and dry. *Always* have alternate plans just in case it happens. Understand, too, that even though famous people *appear* to have all the money they could possibly spend, they often don't and they like to get paid. If you can afford it or your event will make a lot of extra money if your star's appearance is guaranteed, pay the star. Draw up a contract that binds him to appear. He'll show up.

★　★　★

The Incident. It was my great fortune to arrange a fund raising dinner party in Los Angeles celebrating the birthday of the most famous woman of her time—proceeds for cancer research. She's dead now, but the evening lives on in the memory of the 2,100 people who attended. The chairman of the event was a handsome, brilliant banker and philanthropist, and a fine speaker. What I didn't know was that he was in awe of the famous lady and terrified he might say or do something wrong to ruin the evening. So he fortified himself in advance with martinis. When he got to the microphone to greet the audience he was so drunk he had to hang on to keep from falling. It was a humiliating experience for the famous woman, the audience, and me. It was a devastating experience for the chairman. I still get a cold chill when I think about it.

LESSON. Find out everything you can about the people who will be the spokesmen for your project—those who will appear in public on your behalf. Not just whether they drink too much once in a while, but other things. They must be above reproach, with unblemished reputations. A hint of scandal—private, public, or business—can wreck you if it involves people who are closely identified with your project. And of course, at the cocktail party preceding your big dinner, keep your eye on the chairman and the speakers. Both eyes. Assign a committee member to escort each speaker to the event, through the reception, and up to the dais.

★ ★ ★

The Incident. During a college campaign I arranged for the college president to have lunch with the father of one of the students. The father was a wealthy businessman and a prime prospect for a large contribution—I estimated $25,000. The father was very proud of his student son and he brought the boy along to lunch. I suspect he wanted to show his son how important he was—college presidents called on *him*. The lunch was fine and everything was going smoothly until the boy asked the president why one of his favorite teachers had not been given a contract for the coming year. All hell broke loose. The easygoing, sleepy-eyed president turned into a shouting, table-thumping, self-righteous defender of academic discipline. He attacked the terrified boy, who became so frightened he was ready to flee. Do I have to add we didn't get the $25,000?

LESSON. Be mature in your attitude toward your project. If it's attacked, try to avoid a public defense. Your defense will only call further attention to the attack and will give people another reason not to contribute—you're controversial. They'll wonder why you feel you *have* to defend yourself; maybe you are what your attackers say you are. If your project is attacked, *never* counterattack. If the president of the hunting club calls your conservation project a bunch of little old ladies in tennis shoes, don't call his club members killers. Make your case *for your project,* not against your detractors.

My sleepy-eyed college president lost his composure at a critical time. Don't lose yours.

★ ★ ★

The Incident. Early in my fund raising career I worked on a community project in Toronto, Canada. All of our plans were geared to a ten-day period of frantic activity for which we had scheduled dozens of meetings. I was in charge of eighteen luncheons, breakfasts, and dinners, all fund raising meetings. It was an exciting time. On the sixth evening of the ten-day burst I arrived my usual half-hour early at the home of a dinner-party host to check on the arrangements and go over any last-minute questions. The maid let me in and I saw the caterers busily setting tables and preparing food. But I didn't see the host. He and his wife had gone out to dinner! They had forgotten about their party. My secretary had arranged for the caterer but I had forgotten to remind the host, and the host had forgotten to invite anybody.

LESSON. Maybe there are *some* conditions where keeping track of details is unimportant. Fund raising isn't one of them. Nothing is too small to ignore in a campaign. And to insure yourself against forgetting important as well as minor details, do what I do now. I keep a large calendar book that has one page for each day of the year. I write down everything I have to do today on today's page—people I must call, letters I have to write, deadlines I have to meet. There will be a note on the page when I look at it today—I wrote it two weeks ago. It tells me to call Henry because he'll have the answer to something I asked him. Notes about things I can't get done today but aren't pressing are transferred to tomorrow's page. I keep the items on the page in three columns: one is a must-do column, two is a could-wait, and three is minor. Often the items in column three take care of themselves.

I also keep a file in a deep desk drawer. It's one of those accordion things with thirty-one slot-pockets in it, one pocket for each day of the month. That's where I put letters that have to be answered, long notes to myself that won't fit my calendar book, bills that have to be paid, etc. Every day I look into the slot with today's date on it and do what has to be done. Keep track of details; it pays.

★   ★   ★

The Incident.   The most complete direct-mail fund raising campaign ever done in the United States was the project of a former colleague. A famous American had died and a memorial committee was quickly formed. They decided every mailbox in the country should have a letter in it asking for a contribution in memory of the late famous person. Postal authorities and unions agreed to handle the mail free. A massive publicity campaign was conducted. Nothing was left out for this one-time appeal. They weren't sure exactly how much they would raise, but they expected millions. When the last return envelope was opened, they found they had spent more than they had raised.

LESSON.   Raising money in memory of a dead hero is a

tricky business. Raising money through the mails is even trickier. If possible, avoid both.

★ ★ ★

The Incident. I was working in Houston, Texas, on a community-wide project when a rather shabby-looking lady in a moth-eaten coat walked into the office and asked for me. I was busy with all sorts of pressing problems, the phones were ringing, and my head ached. I was tempted to put her off and avoid what looked like a waste of my time. I didn't. She told me she felt I was working on a wonderful project and wanted to help too. She reached into her purse and took out some papers that turned out to be stock certificates worth $20,000. She contributed all of them to the campaign.

LESSON. Never judge a book by its cover? Let's make that: In fund raising always find time to talk to people who want to talk to you about your campaign. That little lady could have taken two hours asking me foolish questions or she could have contributed $2.48 in pennies. It was my job to talk to her. I should never have hesitated, because the project I was working on—and yours, too—was for *people*. When you lose sight of people in your rush to do things for your project, you have lost everything. Don't become a slave to your project. Take time to have fun, smell the flowers, and talk to ladies in shabby coats.

★ ★ ★

The Incident. It had taken me weeks to organize and set the date of a planning meeting for a new campaign I was working on in Dallas, Texas. A prominent business-man had agreed to serve as chairman and we had invited a group to his home. The men who had agreed to attend the planning meeting knew little or nothing about the new project; they were coming to the meeting because the chairman was a man they respected—he had clout. We would have to convince them about the project during the meeting, but I was sure it wouldn't be difficult.

On the day of the meeting the chairman asked if it would be all right for him to invite another guest, an out-of-town visitor. I couldn't think of any possible harm it would do—in fact, I thought it would add to the meeting—so I said yes. I neglected to ask who the visitor was.

He turned out to be the director of another campaign that was looking for Texas support. While the project wasn't competitive with mine, it was glamorous and better known, and it had national prestige. The visitor enlisted everyone at the meeting for his campaign. I had to start over again.

LESSON. If you don't know everybody who's coming to a meeting (*any* kind of meeting, planning, fund raising, brainstorming, victory party), you may be in for unpleasant surprises. If you aren't prepared for any and every possible turn of events at a meeting, you won't know how to handle them if they occur. (I should have visited every guest in advance of the meeting in Dallas and I should have known who the visitor was before he captured my group. My inexperience was my downfall.)

★ ★ ★

The Incident. The project was a hospital in Tulsa, Oklahoma. We had gathered a group of ten top prospects to hear about our campaign and we arranged for a well-known hospital expert to make our case. He was superb. I learned more about hospitals from his thirty-minute talk than I had from months of working on the campaign. Facts and figures, case histories, tragedies, and heartwarming stories poured out in a sequence that led to an inspiring finish. One of the guests, our richest prospect, was so moved by the talk he got up and announced a huge pledge—to a hospital where his mother had died in another city.

LESSON. Our speaker talked about "hospitals" but didn't stress *our* hospital. He made his case too general— there was no compelling reason for our prospects to give to *our* hospital.

Conservation is important, but saving your local bird sanctuary is *your* project. Education is necessary, but *your* school is your project. Medical research is vital, but your cancer facility is *your* project.

Make your case for the campaign you are working on. Let other people save the world—you save your part of it.

★   ★   ★

If you were to squeeze these examples very hard, this is what you would have left:

Know your people.
Pay attention to details.
Plan carefully and be prepared for anything.
Talk and act like a mature adult.
Know your project and stick to it.
Something free can be very expensive.
Let the departed rest in peace.
Take time to smell the flowers.

10

Fund Raising Methods, Events, and Tactics: Acronyms to Zip Codes

Everybody who raises money schedules some kind of special event sooner or later.

There are good reasons to have an event as part of your fund raising. The event calls attention to your project; it gives your committee a target to work toward; for those in your group who will never be comfortable asking people for money, the event serves as a substitute—they can sell the event rather than the cause; an event can uncover hidden constituents. On the other hand, some events may have no bearing on your project and people won't remember why they came in the first place; by attending an event some prospects may go away with the feeling they helped you somehow, and a $50 ticket sale may be all you'll get from a $500 prospect.

Be careful in your choice of event, method, or tactic. Because I describe one doesn't mean I'm in favor of it. You won't have any trouble finding out the ones I recommend or those I oppose. However, you, your group, and your project may be the perfect combination that can perform miracles, and I wouldn't want to stand in the way of a miracle. So try anything you think will make money for you.

But before you do, ask yourself these questions—they

could be the critical difference between choosing the right or wrong special event.

1. If you were a prospect for your campaign, would you go to the special event?

2. If you were a prospect, would you give the same amount of money without the event? Why?

3. If you were *not* involved in your campaign, how would you feel about the event? Uninterested? Critical? Enthusiastic? Bored?

4. How will those you are trying to help feel about it? Embarrassed? Proud? Nothing?

5. Will the event tend to obscure the purpose of your organization—when it's over, will people remember the project as well as the event?

6. Is the event so woven into the fabric of your organization that nobody else could use it?

7. Is there a simpler, less expensive, more effective event you can use?

8. Can the event become an annual, looked-forward-to project that can be improved each year?

9. Is your event dependent on things you can't control, like good weather? Movie stars? Popular politicians?

10. Could your event succeed without a word of publicity? Or are you counting on a mass communications media blitz, another factor you can't control?

11. Are you counting upon people buying tickets at the door, another risky condition you can't control?

You should be pretty clear in your mind about what your special event should do for you besides raise some money and get you a little coverage in the mass communications media. Here's a short list of special event objectives. If your special event can accomplish two or more of them, you may have a really good one. If not, go back and plan a different event.

1. Your event should reinforce the dedication of your campaign and project leaders.
2. Your event should attract some new, potential leaders.
3. Your event should develop new donors who can be approached in the future.
4. Your event should upgrade current donors from one level of giving to a higher level.
5. Your event should train and educate old and new leaders about your project, and make them glad they're a part of what you are doing.

I have listed the various methods, events, and tactics alphabetically, so you're bound to find one that fits your current condition and needs. If you decide to use one of the methods I talk about, be sure to test it before you plunge in. Testing will eliminate any unexpected bugs. It will show you the possible pitfalls you could run into when you are ready to go all out. Your whole approach could be wrong and people will tell you. You may see the value in using postage-free return envelopes instead of making prospects buy a stamp—or the other way round. Use the test the way businessmen and politicians use surveys—to find out if their products or candidates can be sold, and if not, why not. Test small. If it fails, you won't have invested a lot of money. In politics, 1,500 samples can predict the new governor, and you can predict how well you'll do with fewer samples than 1,500.

ACRONYMS. A word made from the first letter of other words is an acronym. Northern Ungawa Termite Society = NUTS. Many new organizations twist themselves into pretzel shapes to come up with a name that will make a smashing acronym. If you're new and trying it, abandon it. But you think it will give you instant recognition to be called SCARE or BOW-WOW or FOOT. You're right, but you're still going to have to explain what your cute acronym stands for. The NAACP doesn't need translation. You know what it means because the NAACP program and activities are known to you.

Acronyms are like slogans. People waste time trying to think of nifty ones because other groups use them when they should be concerned about important matters. Some acronyms are silly, others are corny and contrived, and they have never persuaded anybody to give money away.

Be different. If you're a new group, choose a *name*, not an acronym.

ART SHOWS. There are many talented amateur and good unknown professional artists who would welcome a chance to be exhibited. Give them that chance and raise money too. Talk to art dealers and art teachers and find out who the artists are. Make arrangements with them about frames and price. Build in a profit for your project that will make all the work worthwhile. See if a local art gallery will cooperate and serve as the showplace. Or try the local library or college. An open-air show on a Sunday afternoon in a parking lot could attract passing traffic. But you'll have to do a lot of drumbeating to get a crowd for an art show. So test it by getting eight or ten pictures and show them in a private home with twenty to thirty prospective buyers invited.

Beware of promoters who would dearly love to pass off fifth- and sixth-rate art junk on you and your friends if you play patsy for them.

AUCTIONS. In some cities there are so many charity

auctions that you practically can't buy anything retail anymore, so your competition will be great. Don't do what everybody else is doing or you'll get lost. The obvious elements in an auction are: the crowd, the location of the auction, the items to be sold, and the auctioneer. Try to avoid hodgepodge auctions where you sell toasters and sculpture. Stick to a category that will attract a specific kind of buyer—works of art or appliances or furniture, not all at the same time. Then bombard your potential buyers with notices, invitations, phone calls. *Get* them there.

Plan the location of the auction carefully. Be sure it's centrally located for your buyers, with lots of parking space.

Give yourself plenty of planning time; it may take longer than you think to get your items together, stored, priced, insured, catalogued, and moved.

Don't leave the auctioneering job to an amateur, no matter how hard he worked on your committee. If you can't get a professional auctioneer to run your sale, at least talk to one and get his advice. Auctioneering is a highly skilled art and you could lose months of hard work with the wrong person wielding the hammer. The professional will tell you what you need to know about pace, shills, price, timing, and so on.

In many big cities, art galleries and antique shops will run an auction for you. They provide everything: items, location, auctioneer. You provide the potential buyers from your group and the gallery gives you a percentage of the sale—sometimes as much as 30 percent. Be careful. The items offered by the gallery could be stuff they can't get rid of any other way and your people may get stuck with second-rate items at inflated prices.

Another word of caution about auctions: If someone buys a $20 toaster at your auction for $15, he cannot take a charitable tax deduction! The Internal Revenue Service is very clear on that point. If you get something in return for your contribution—a meal, a cake, a toaster, a yacht, or anything—you can deduct ony the amount of your contribution over and above the value of what you got in return. If you paid $100 for a painting that is appraised at $80, you can deduct $20 as a charitable gift. If you paid $80 for a $100 painting, all you get is the painting.

Running a charity auction can be fun if you use your imagination. I once ran an auction of gifts from famous people with signed letters from them to show the gift was authentic. The gifts were highly personal: a pair of dancing slippers from a world-famous ballerina, an original page from a symphony score by a famous composer, a complete set of autographed books by a noted author, and so on. The items had collectors' and sentimental value and we charged $100 per person admission to a black-tie dinner for the privilege of bidding, with proceeds for cancer research.

The items you sell could be symbolic—a bed at the local children's hospital, two hundred books for the college library, leg braces for crippled children, and so on. The symbolic auction eliminates the need to collect salable items and is more in the tradition of philanthropy than selling a toaster. In addition, you can sell more than one set of leg braces or hospital beds and your buyer gets a total tax deduction.

You don't have to have a Rembrandt painting or two hundred millionaires in a room to test your auction. The symbolic auction, of course, needs nothing but buyers. Other auctions can be tested by gathering a few items, waffle irons, twenty-pound cartons of soap flakes, dinner for two at a local restaurant, all donated by local merchants. Invite thirty or forty people and see what happens. When you are finished, you'll know how to run a larger auction, or whether you should have one in the first place.

You might even try to collect two or three expensive items and have twenty or thirty bidders rich enough to compete against each other. Whatever you do, do it small but thoroughly.

BAKE SALES. This traditional method of raising small sums of money for worthy causes is as old as the discovery of wheat. There is nothing I can tell you about a bake sale you don't already know. Except this: Put a twist into your bake sale. Ask the governor's wife to bake a cake for your sale. Or ask the governor! The mayor? Have all of your cakes and pies baked by the most famous people you can reach. Then invite *their* friends and supporters to the sale.

Hide expensive watches or jewelry in some of the baked goods and let people know they have a chance to be like Jack Horner and pull out a plum from the pie. Then raise the price of each pie. Get the mayor or somebody famous to go to the home of a big contributor to bake his cake.

A bake sale doesn't have to be tested, obviously. But if you are going to try to run one that's different, it might be a good idea to do it small first.

BENEFITS.   See Galas.

BEQUESTS.   See Wills.

BINGO.   Do I have to explain? Only church groups in some areas are allowed to have bingo parties. If you fit, see Gambling for another way of raising money from people who like the thrill of games of chance.

I recently consulted with a group that raised most of its money from bingo—more than $150,000 per year. That's right! I cautioned them that bingo players are not loyal donors, they're gamblers. If there's a storm the night of the weekly bingo game, they won't mail in a check for the money they would have lost. Or if someone else opens up a bingo game closer to their home, they'll abandon the old one without a second thought.

I recommended that they continue their bingo game, of course, but develop a strong board and committee and constituency as soon as possible.

I don't want you to think my clients routinely ignore my advice, but this one did. A competing bingo game took away many of their players so they had to cut back on several of their charitable programs. With no other regular fund raising to fall back on, they finally closed their doors.

BOOK SALES. Not recommended. They don't raise a lot of money, lots of nice people work very hard, other people get rid of books they don't want because they were gathering dust, and there's never a Shakespeare first folio or an autographed Dickens—or an autographed anything, for that matter. I'm not sure I understand why people bother with book sales unless they enjoy the social benefits of working together. That's fine, but it just isn't good fund raising unless you gather an array of expensive books, or old books of value, or beautifully bound books, and have an appreciative, wealthy group of buyers.

CARD CALLING. It goes by different names in different places, but it means the same: You gather a group of prospects in one place, you call out their names and ask them to make pledges. It can be embarrassing for the giver and the asker, but it's the most effective fund raising method ever devised with the possible exception of Eyeball-to-Eyeball. Some people think it's crude and vulgar and maybe it is, but not long ago I was present when card calling was used at the residence of then Cardinal Mc-

Intyre, with the Cardinal present. It was effective, and an old children's hospital was remodeled as a result.

The most important thing to know about card calling is when to use it and how. Be sure everybody you gather together knows in advance they're going to be asked for money. All it takes is one surprised, irate prospect to destroy the pitch. Be sure everybody you gather knows about and approves of your project. Be sure at least one-third of your group has been seen in advance and has made a pledge. Be sure the one who makes the pitch is a good, confident speaker, is known and respected by the group, and makes his own gift first! And be sure his own gift is big enough so everybody knows he made a sacrifice.

Be sure your speaker (who can be the pitchman, too) can inspire the group. It can be low-key or table-thumping so long as it's inspirational. Be sure the one who makes the pitch is patient—very patient. People may respond slowly and your man will have to sense the tempo.

Be sure you call the names in a sequence that will get the best results. Don't call a $5,000 prospect right after a $200 pledge. Mix your prepledge names judiciously—and get a few of them in early.

Card calling works. It works for big contributions or small ones. And it has a marvelous, almost mystical effect upon even the most reluctant prospect. Test it on a small group of about ten or twelve and you'll see that I am right.

(For a gentler method, see Open Pledges.)

CHALLENGE GIFTS. Some foundations and a few so-phisticated philanthropists use the challenge gift method, and it's a good one. Here's how it works: If your goal is, for example, $300,000, they'll give the *last* $50,000. It's not like a matching gift, because you get nothing if you don't raise the first $250,000. In a matching gift arrangement, you get a dollar or two or three for every dollar you raise. Or vice versa—you get one dollar for every three you raise. A challenge gift can be a great stimulus toward the end of a campaign. As you begin to approach the amount you have to raise in order to collect on the challenge, the thought of losing the challenge gift acts as a spur to your committee and it becomes a marvelous selling argument to your prospects.

Do you have a skeptical prospect on your list? Someone who doesn't believe you can raise the money you need but would help you if other people did? The challenge gift tactic might work with him. Incidentally, you can arrange for more than one challenge gift, and space them at strategic points toward your goal.

COIN BOX. Don't use it. I don't care who else does, it will reduce your campaign to the level of pennies and dimes. Don't even test it.

CONCERTS. Rock concerts, symphony concerts, concerts starring one famous performer are not recommended unless you are in an organization with lots of dedicated people who can go out and sell tickets by the hundreds and thousands.

A client I counseled persuaded Sammy Davis, Jr., to perform at a one-man concert. They were going to rent an outdoor auditorium with 15,000 seats. It could have turned out to be a nightmare because there were only a few people connected with the institution who were willing to sell tickets. Rental on the auditorium and advertising expenses would have been astronomical. With luck they might have come out even. I persuaded them to get their richest donor to play host to Sammy Davis, Jr. We rented a large tent and had it installed on the grounds of the donor's house. He invited *his* rich friends to an exclusive evening with Sammy Davis, Jr. Sammy Davis, Jr., was phenomenal. Halfway through the performance he stopped and cajoled $236,000 out of the delighted audience, then he performed special requests until midnight. We spent $900 for the tent and champagne.

Didn't I say I don't recommend concerts? Yes. If you have to sell a lot of tickets and don't have the manpower, forget them. Don't rely on advertising or the drawing power of famous performers. Some celebrities will cancel a benefit performance in favor of a paying one and they'll leave you holding an expensive contract with musicians, auditoriums, printers, and advertising people.

But you want to *try* a concert, they look like fun, and other people do them. Okay. Try a small one. Get talented and not-so-talented kids to put together a show. Then sell tickets to their adoring families. Otherwise, forget it.

Sure, the Toronto Symphony scheduled the late Jack Benny to play the violin and packed the halls. But the Toronto Symphony has a hall of its own, paid musicians under contract, an influential board of trustees who can buy and sell tickets, *and* a ready-made audience that regularly buys tickets no matter what the program might be.

CONVOCATIONS: It literally means "a calling together." And that's what you do: You call together a group, large or small, to spend a day or two talking about your project. You provide the site and one, two, or more experts in your field as speakers. They speak, your group asks questions, and the dialogue follows. If the convocation lasts a full day or longer, the prospects you invited will have a chance to rub elbows with your experts, learn more about your project, and be softened when you are ready to ask for their gifts.

For organizations that are well known, a convocation can be an excellent event. For those not well known, it can be a way of introducing you to your potential givers in an unrushed atmosphere that treats them as more than walking dollar signs.

Let me show you how a convocation works. The project is a mental health clinic. It needs $100,000 for additional staff and some remodeling. The first speaker is a well-known psychologist. His subject: Recognizing Mental Illness in Children. The second speaker is a psychiatric case worker. Subject: Family Conditions in a Home with a Retarded Person. The audience: the prospect list of the clinic plus anybody else they can think of. Time: Saturday, 10 A.M. to lunch (charge $6.50); 1:30 P.M. to 4 P.M. Place: the clinic itself or the faculty club of the local college. Moderator: the head man at the clinic. Closing speaker: the fund raising chairman or the best pitchman on the committee. The committee members work like beavers to get their prospects to attend. Printed material about the clinic is available for all guests. Fund raising method: choose among Eyeball-to-Eyeball right after the convocation or the next day; Card Calling; Open Pledges.

There must be something your project is doing that people would like to hear about from an expert—the more famous the expert, the better. Give your prospects a chance to see your organization in a new or different light; you'll both come away refreshed. But test it out first with one speaker and twenty guests sitting around the table. The test could have a fringe benefit: with only twenty guests you can concentrate on those prospects you might want to recruit for your committee.

DINNERS, PER-PLATE.   A per-plate dinner, of course, is one where you sell tickets to the dinner for $50 each, or $100, or $1,000, or more. Although there are many shortcomings to per-plate dinners, I recommend them most of the time. Here are some of the drawbacks: everybody pays the same amount, rich and not so rich, unless your rich prospect buys a table of ten seats; if you don't charge enough per plate, costs can reduce your profit drastically; people who buy dinner tickets feel they have made their contribution, no matter what your rating says they could give.

If your per-plate dinner becomes a yearly event, it could be used to reach prospects you haven't seen up to that time, and the money you raise can help to decide next year's goal—annual per-plate dinners usually get a little bigger each year. If your dinner sells many tickets, you will have an impressive number to show your top prospects who may want to know how many others are giving.

Please don't expect people to come to a per-plate dinner just because you mailed them an invitation. Your committee will have to see prospects and call them. Yes, you can use the phone this time because you'll have to reach hundreds to get dozens.

I won't go into the details of a per-plate dinner because the Event Checklist in the Appendix covers everything you'll have to do. I will caution you again about how much to charge. The arithmetic is simple—500 people at $100 per plate is $50,000. Costs will be between $7,000 and $50,000 or more, depending upon what part of the country you live in, what you serve, printing costs, staff, speakers' fees, etc.

The comedian Pat Paulsen once put on an 89-cents-a-plate spaghetti testimonial dinner to himself at a cafeteria when he ran for president. It was a funny publicity stunt but you're not in a funny enterprise. Don't charge $50 per plate if food will cost $25 and other expenses like flowers, taxes and tips will add $15 per person. A $10 profit on a $50 item may be great for a business, but not for you.

Test a per-plate dinner this way: Call a meeting of your inner group. Explain the per-plate event and ask each one how many *tables of ten* he will buy. Then ask how many *tables of ten* he thinks he can sell to prospects. Estimate the number of additional per-plate tickets you can sell by mail to other prospects, corporations, and businesses in your area. Be realistic in your estimate. Now add the numbers and cut 25 percent from your total. That's about how many plates you will sell.

DOOR-TO-DOOR.   This is the standby method for some campaigns and the major source of funds for several others. What stinker could turn down a child in a Halloween costume who rings his doorbell? Or who could refuse to buy a box of Girl Scout cookies? Door-to-door campaigns require a huge volunteer group and I don't recommend door-to-door campaigns unless you have an army of askers standing by. Door-to-door is an easy method to test because you're in complete control. Pick out a small target—a few blocks or so. Inundate those blocks with literature in advance. Let the people know that on the arranged date someone will be ringing their doorbells on behalf of your project. Many people don't answer their doorbells at night anymore, so do it in the daytime and be sure you don't frighten the prospects! Because you're working on a relatively small scale, you can train your doorbell ringers on how to act and what to say. If the test fails, your investment was small. If it succeeds, the city could be yours.

EYEBALL-TO-EYEBALL.   Sounds menacing, doesn't it? I've talked about it before as face-to-face fund raising where somebody asks somebody else for a contribution. I could have used cornering, putting the bite or the bee on, clouting, nailing, or a dozen other expressions. I like eyeball-to-eyeball because it makes you equal to your prospect—you and he are talking to and looking at each other as peers. Nobody's begging, and nobody's having his arm twisted. It is *the one best way to raise money.* All you have to do is arrange to see your prospect, explain your campaign to him, tell him how much you're giving, and ask him for his gift after you tell him how much you expect of him. He'll say either yes, no, that's too much, or I'll have to think about it. He may make excuses, change the subject, arrange to talk to his partner or his wife first, or say all sorts of other things. You keep bringing the subject back to his gift. It's really very simple for you. It's simple for him, too, if he agrees. Otherwise, he has to go through mental gymnastics that can be exhausting.

If there was a better way to raise money, I'd tell you about it. Honest.

FASHION SHOWS. Another method particularly suited to women's groups. If you're in a large metropolitan area and your group has a large membership, you may get a noted fashion designer to work with you. You raise money by charging admission to the show, or you have the show at a luncheon and you sell luncheon tickets at a profit. Fashion shows can be very expensive and I don't recommend them unless you do everything yourself: Your group designs the clothes, models them, and sells tickets. At best, you'll have a good time and make a little money.

FLEA MARKETS. The women's support group of a large college in California has an annual flea market. For months they collect things from attics, from friends, from businesses, from manufacturers. Some of it is plain junk, some of it is fancy junk, and some is useful—sweaters, cans of tuna fish, fabrics. They set up tables at a huge parking lot and sell everything at bargain prices. And they raise a lot of money, which always surprises me. Flea markets or junk sales work only if you have a large group of hard-working people who will stick with you all the way. Otherwise, I don't recommend them for anybody. The problems can overwhelm you, and are much the same kinds of problems you would have to deal with in an auction, except you'll have more of them: collecting items, storage, carting, pricing, records, publicity (you'll need it for a big flea market), advertising, printing, security, parking, setting up and tearing down the sales tables, keeping track of checks and cash, and more. A small flea market would be the best way to start, if you are determined to try one. Since it's small, you can be a little more selective in the kind of stuff you accept. So you might select only fabrics and small knickknacks; they're lightweight and won't take up much storage room. By trying a small one you'll learn more about a big one than I could possibly teach you. Remember, the person who gives you the merchandise gets the tax deduction, the one who buys it doesn't.

FOLLOW-UP. Follow-up is not an event, a method, or even a tactic. It's one of the most important terms in fund raising and the most used and abused. Of course you follow up every lead, every prospect, every foundation, every opportunity. Attention to the smallest detail, the most insignificant opening pays off. Then there comes a time when you must ask for the contribution or all your hard work will be wasted.

Many of the events I describe are for fund raising, not for educating people about your cause. If you work very hard and get several hundred people to your event and *don't* ask them for their contributions, you have done your project a disservice. The *event* is the follow-up. How can you possibly recapture the feeling created by a great speaker when you talk to your prospect three days later? How can you see and talk to everybody who attended? It could take weeks or months to follow up on, say, two hundred people. Do you dare risk everything you've worked for in the hope your guests will mail their gifts to you? I can tell you flatly it won't work. Yes, some people will take home an envelope and mail you a check; but only a few, and they won't give as much as they would have at the event.

The term follow-up is abused when reluctant askers postpone the asking. They can postpone your project out of existence by following up and never closing in.

GALAS. The nightmare of the professional fund raiser, the darling of the society editors. The star-studded event that makes the morning edition and little else. Grown people behave like infants when they try to decide whether this year's gala should have "elephants and apes" as the theme or just plain "apes." Whether the basic color in the ballroom should be puce or tangerine. Rock music or waltzes, or both. People seem to lose sight of the orphans or crippled children who are supposed to benefit when they argue between filet mignon and quail as the main course on the gala menu. And please don't tell me about such-and-such a group that raises a fortune every year at their masked ball, or Miss Movie Star's annual half-million-dollar charity show. I know all about them, including how much they cost and how much time they take to put together.

If your cause is so flimsy the only way to raise money for it is by having a gala, I suppose you'll have one no matter what I say. But a project that has any validity at all can raise money with less expense. I could be facetious and suggest you sell tickets to a non-gala: For $100 a couple, people don't have to attend anything—they can stay at home and talk to each other.

Please understand the galas I'm against are those for so-called worthy causes. Social gatherings to celebrate an anniversary or a new ambassador are not on my no-no list.

Benefits, events to raise money for an individual in dire need, fall into the gala category. There are many better ways to raise the money you need. If a benefit fails it could be a disaster.

GAMBLING. A gambling event can be tricky. If the laws in your area allow it, it works like this: You set up roulette wheels, dice tables, blackjack tables, and whatever gambling games you want to try. Your guests buy chips and use those chips to gamble at your tables. Or you can take them out on a boat beyond the three-mile limit (check with your police chief).

I don't recommend gambling of any kind as a fund raising device. Aside from the moral considerations, you risk losing money at a gambling event and your project risks losing its image.

GARAGE SALES. See Flea Markets. (And add everything you and your group have lying around your houses you want to get rid of.)

GIMMICKS. Walkathons, jumping-frog contests, wrestling matches with a trained bear, and other gimmicks have mushroomed as competition for the small gift has grown. I don't like gimmick fund raising and I don't recommend it for a reason I've given before: the gimmick replaces the project in people's minds. The frog becomes more important than the cause you are raising the money for. There is no way I can stop somebody in your group from dreaming up a gimmick and trying to force it on your campaign. So, when it happens, don't treat it like the invention of the wheel. Kick it, prod it, laugh at it, ridicule it, and try to kill it. If it's still alive, examine it to see if it's a better fund raising method than *any* other you can use. Will it take people's eyes off the ball—your project? Will it distract your inner-group members from doing what they should do—seeing prospects? Some gimmicks are cute as can be and others may look like the answer to your campaign prayers. Don't fall for them. They are usually Sirens who will lure you to possible destruction.

HOUSE PARTIES. A house party can be useful if your prospects aren't very rich, or if your goal isn't very big, or if your project isn't a high-priority one. A house party is what it says it is, a party in somebody's house, with the difference: Guests pay for food and drinks. They can be huge (I went to one at a mansion with a thousand people) or modest, indoors or on the lawn, Saturday or Sunday, lunchtime or cocktail hour or dinner. At some point in the party somebody should speak for five or ten minutes about your project so people will know why they are there. Food and drinks can be provided by the committee, or bought and the committee can serve, or you can hire servants. A house party could be an event to use to recruit new committee people. And it might provide a relaxed atmosphere for preliminary talks with major prospects.

If you know in advance what you want to accomplish, this old method, the house party, can help you do it. You don't even have to test it unless you're planning a giant one for the future.

INTENT, LETTERS OF. I am always surprised at how few letters of intent are on file at the headquarters of large institutions that have wealthy donors and trustees. The letter of intent says simply, I intend to leave you something when I die. The "something" can be spelled out or not, depending upon the circumstances.

If yours is a project that is going to be around for a long time, you should have a letter of intent from every member of your inner group. It doesn't matter how poor they are, everybody leaves something.

A letter of intent is not a will. It does not have to be drawn up by a lawyer and it doesn't have to be signed by a witness or a notary. It's just a letter, and it's not binding upon the estate of the man who signs it. What good is it? It makes the man who signs it think about drawing up a will or adding the intent to the will if one exists. Discussing a letter of intent is not like discussing a will. It doesn't have the same connotation, somehow. Most people consider their wills to be their own business, not open for discussion with anybody but their attorneys. But they may be willing to talk about a letter of intent.

Other people do not have a will for superstitious reasons or because they're waiting for the right time to draw one up, whenever that might be. In each case, a letter of intent can be the way you open the door for your project to become a beneficiary of their generosity.

Do I have to emphasize delicacy, restraint, and gentleness in your approach to prospects for a letter of intent?

By all means, test your technique before you launch an inner-group intent campaign. Talk to two or three of the most dedicated people first. Enlist their help in devising an approach to others. Point out how valuable it would be for them to draw up intent letters you could use as examples. Do your own first.

JOURNALS, SOUVENIR. Almost as old as printing, the souvenir journal is a way to raise money for your project and give your prospect a business deduction that is usually better for him than a charitable one. At the same time, you'd better be careful how you handle the reporting of journal income. If you use this method, talk to your lawyer.

On the chance you've never worked on a souvenir journal, here's one example out of thousands of possible variations.

Project: $30,000 to remodel and refurnish the Sunday-school building on your church grounds. Church membership: 500 families. Date of campaign victory party: ninety days hence.

A reliable printer quotes a figure of $4,000 for 500 copies of a 100-page magazine about the size of *Newsweek*. Twenty pages will be copy you provide about the Sunday school, ten pages about the church, and seventy pages reserved for advertising. With luck, fifty pages will be sold at rates of $200 a full page, $125 a half page, $75 for one-quarter page, and $40 for one-eighth page.

Local merchants, businessmen, and nonchurch-member friends are asked to "buy" a message or advertisement that will gain them the respect and friendship of every member of the church. The "buyer" provides advertising copy and pays extra—your cost—for color plates.

Fifty pages of ads at an average income of $250 per page will net $8,500 from sources outside the church membership.

I don't recommend journals except for those closed-constituency campaigns like churches and service clubs. And then only if the goal is small and you use the method sparingly—never more than once a year.

Before you commit your organization to a printing bill you'll get stuck with, talk to a few journal prospects and get their commitment. If you can sell ten pages easily, go ahead. Otherwise, give the money back.

KIND, GIFTS IN. Sure, you know what they are: free carpeting from a company for your day-school project; free office space; free use of a truck to pick up items for your auction or flea market. A gift in kind is one time you *should* look a gift horse in the mouth. What are you getting? A truck that needs a $400 repair job before it will run? An office you wouldn't use under any circumstances? Moth-eaten carpeting that will cost you a fortune to install?

I was once offered $200,000 worth of unexposed film for a university client with a motion picture department. It looked like a bonanza until an expert examined the film and told us it wasn't any good.

Some people are eager to take a full tax write-off for gifts in kind you wouldn't pass on to your worst enemy.

Obviously not all—not even most—gifts in kind are tax dodges or useless. Some of the most brilliant advertising ideas for charities have been created by agencies donating their services and have appeared free in magazines and newspapers and on television and radio. Many companies have contributed medicines and clothing, goods and services of great value. Consider your project. Are there gifts in kind you really need, things you woud buy if you had the money? Necessities, not luxuries. If your answer is yes, treat the sources of the things you need as though they were dollar prospects and solicit the gifts the same way you would the money. Assign the companies you're after to your best committee member. But don't go after a gift in kind if what you really need is cash—and don't accept a gift in kind unless you're sure you won't get any money.

LADIES. Ladies are neither a fund raising event nor a method. I hope you won't be insulted if I call you a "tactic." In too many campaigns, women are segregated into their "auxiliaries" or another category that removes them from top leadership. It's almost always a mistake, and a costly mistake at that. Not every woman has the combination of skills, personality, and energy to be chairman of a campaign, but neither does every man. Women often have more free time than men, and much of that time may be wasted on campaign chores with little or no dollar return.

Los Angeles has a performing arts complex that is among the best in the world. If you had to choose the one person most responsible for this multimillion-dollar project, you would have to name Mrs. Norman Chandler. True, she's an extraordinary woman and there aren't too many like her, but there aren't too many projects like the Los Angeles Music Center either.

Check your list of inner family and combine the men's and women's committees if they are segregated. Is there a woman who could be chairman? Co-chairman? Do you have a few prospects nobody is anxious to approach? Send your most persuasive women. Most men find it difficult to turn down a reasonable request from someone who takes the trouble to visit them at their offices. They may not *like* it but it's effective.

LETTER JOBS. A letter job is direct-mail fund raising with a difference. Somebody with influence on a lot of people sends them a personal letter asking for money for his project. Somebody like the owner of a furniture outlet writing to the manufacturers who sell to him. A multimillion-dollar national campaign uses this method almost exclusively.

It may look like I'm contradicting myself when I say I recommend letter-job fund raising. Try it, but only if you're sure you can't get your askers to ask face to face. Try it if you have many more prospects than you can possibly see in person. Try it if you are asking your prospects for less than $100—solicit a major gift prospect by letter only when you have exhausted every chance for a meeting with him.

There are a few things you should know that will give your letter-job campaign a good chance of succeeding. Use the stationery of the man who signs the letter—your asker. Don't use a campaign letterhead unless you absolutely have to. The letter should be hand-typed and hand-signed. The asker must know the prospect, preferably by his first name, and the letter is addressed "Dear Paul." Try to find askers with clout—people who hire or buy goods and services rather than people who depend upon others for their income. And, most important of all for letter jobs, ask for a specific amount: "$26.75 will send one child to summer camp for a week-end"; "$18.50 will buy a month's supply of chemicals for the artificial kidney."

Letter jobs are useful when you are in a campaign that goes on year after year. Givers can be asked to give again the second year even though your original asker may have dropped out or moved. The renewal rate is particularly high.

Test the letter-job method with two or three members of your committee as askers. If you get at least a 10-percent return, you're onto something you should expand.

LUNCHEONS. Luncheons are different from dinners in one important way: There's a time limit at lunch. People have to get back to their daily business, so you should be careful when you plan your agenda. Arrange a simple menu—one course plus a simple dessert. Promise your guests they'll be out by 1:30 P.M. or 2:00 P.M. and keep your promise. Everything about the luncheon should be businesslike. Brief presentations and speakers. Everything else about the luncheon is the same as at a dinner.

MATCHING FUNDS. (See also Challenge Gifts.) You've heard about matching funds and I've told you a little about them. It's a great tactic when it's used right. But even more important is getting a matching gift in the first place.

A matching-gift prospect should be someone from whom you're pretty sure you'll get a reasonably good contribution. After you have his pledge—and only then—ask him if he'll give an *additional* amount to be used for matching purposes. Explain how important it will be to your campaign. It might persuade some prospects to give who would have refused and others to give more than they had planned. Ask him if you may use his name when you talk to others about his matching gift. Some prospects may be skeptical about your "anonymous" matching gift and it might lose some of its value.

You may find a prospect who will give *only* if someone else gives—a competitor of his or a friend or a notorious community tightwad. If you don't think you can get that someone else to give, tell your prospect he's much too important to have to resort to personality games and is above that sort of thing. If he won't budge, take him up on his deal and do the best you can.

Use your matching gifts whenever you can, particularly at fund raising meetings where you have a group of prospects present. Your committee members should be armed with the information when they visit their prospects.

Obviously, you should keep track of gifts, you get in response to your matching offer. Foundations will insist on it and individuals should be treated the same way. And if you match a gift quickly, you just might get another. Ask for it.

NEWSPAPER ADS. For a typical campaign—a hospital, Community Chest, health or educational project—newspaper ads are not recommended. For a crisis campaign they may be useful. If they're going to tear down that landmark your group is trying to save, a full-page ad in the paper could arouse the community, raise enough money to pay for the ad with a little left over, and provide you with a quick list of prospects for the future.

Don't try to write the ad yourself. Talk to an advertising agency and let them do it.

If you're going to try a newspaper ad, go full page or nothing. Give your reader a sense of how important your project is by the way it explodes out of the paper at him— not tucked away between a news story and a lingerie sale. A full page in a big city paper is expensive but a quarter page is almost worthless in a fund raising campaign, so don't test small.

Think very hard about taking out that full-page ad and do it only if you have a real, honest-to-goodness critical condition you are trying to correct in a hurry.

OPEN PLEDGES. Right behind Eyeball-to-Eyeball and Card Calling, the most effective fund raising tactic is open pledges. If your prospects are told in advance they will be asked to contribute and they come to the lunch or dinner or party or whatever event you use, open pledges will probably give you maximum results.

In addition to a good speaker and pitchman, you'll need pace, prepledges, and patience.

Pace doesn't mean tempo in this case. It means setting a level of giving that gets the most from your prospects. If the first few announced gifts are small, your major gift prospects may go along with the pace set for them. So always have several major gift prospects prepledged and ready to announce their gifts. (Go back and reread Card Calling because everything is the same except that in card calling, *you* will decide who will make the first pledges by calling on prospects in a sequence you choose.)

More so than in card calling, patience is necessary in open pledge fund raising. Give your prospects all the time they need to make up their minds.

For open pledge fund raising, a smaller gathering of prospects is better than a large one. In a large group, five hundred people at a dinner, for example, prospects may feel remote, the pitch is less personal, the prospect will probably have to fill out a pledge card to be collected and brought to the microphone where it's announced for him, and the feeling of intimacy is lost.

In a smaller group of fifty or less, an open pledge can be heard by everybody, will have a greater impact on others, and will be more satisfying to the giver because it won't be drowned out or ignored and everybody present will know who did what.

I am all too well aware that card calling and open pledge fund raising do not enjoy universal acceptance. That's too mild. Many people hate it is closer to the truth. *Most* people is even closer. I don't have to go into their reasons; we know them. But card calling and open pledging work. They get the most from a prospect, and that's what your project needs.

OPENING NIGHTS. Theaters and movie houses regularly sell the opening night of a potential hit show to an organization, and you have probably bought tickets yourself.

Before you commit your project to an opening night there are many things to consider: Will you be selling a $10 or $20 ticket to a $100 prospect? Will you have enough ticket sellers to fill the house? Will your profits justify the amount of work you will have to do? Can you get the theater free? Many people who buy opening-night tickets for charitable causes don't remember the cause. Do you care? Are there prospects who could buy blocks of seats? Do you have prospects who will buy tickets at very high prices as their contribution to your project? Will those who contributed earlier resent being asked to buy a ticket? Should you use an opening night as the final event of your campaign and give free tickets to all contributors above a certain level?

For reasons of their own, some askers don't mind selling tickets but won't ask for an outright contribution. If your committee is made up of that kind of asker, you may have to use an opening night or another ticket event. Answer my questions first and devise a plan that makes the most money for the effort you will surely put into it. Set your ticket prices as high as you dare. Scale the house—charge more for better seats. If yours is a high-priority project, see if you can get the stars to attend an after-show reception to which you invite special prospects. They might agree if you ask them.

PARLOR MEETINGS. They are just what they say they are, a meeting that takes place in somebody's parlor. Please don't ask me where the name came from, but I can tell you there are many campaigns that don't really need any other method. Parlor meetings are simple to run, effective, inexpensive, and lend themselves to the three best fund raising tactics: Eyeball-to-Eyeball, Card Calling, and Open Pledges.

Here's how they work: Someone close to your project invites a group of potential donors to his home. They should be people he knows well, but they don't have to be, so long as they are good prospects. Dinner is best, but a Sunday brunch or lunch or after-dinner dessert and coffee can work, too. All the guests know why they are invited so nobody can claim the fund raising came as a surprise. The atmosphere at home is friendly, people are relaxed, and unless somebody commits a horrible gaffe, you almost can't prevent money from being raised.

You should have an effective speaker who can tell the guests about your project in a clear and compelling way. The host makes the pitch for funds—he has to, it's his home and they're his guests. And that's it. There are two things you will have to decide: how many people should be invited and whether to invite husbands *and* wives. The ideal parlor meeting has about fifteen prospects, and since it's a fund raising setting, it may or may not be better for the campaign to invite wives. It depends upon how your community handles these things.

A typical agenda for a parlor meeting looks like this:

1. Dinner.
2. The group moves to a room where all can sit comfortably and face the speaker.
3. The host welcomes the guests and thanks them for showing their interest in the project by accepting his invitation.
4. The host may say a few words about the project and then introduce the speaker.
5. The speaker talks about the project for about thirty minutes, never more than forty-five minutes.
6. The host thanks the speaker and goes right into the fund raising tactic agreed upon in advance.
7. After the fund raising, the host thanks his guests again and may suggest they stay for further discussion with the speaker.

When parlor meetings break down it's usually between agenda numbers 5 and 6. A modest or fearful host may change his mind when he's finally confronted with the job of asking for money. Be prepared for that to happen. If it does, you should have someone ready to start things off with a pledge. That kind of support often gives the timorous host the courage he needs to carry on.

Between numbers 5 and 6, somebody may ask a question of the speaker or the host. If you stop to answer the question your good manners could reduce your fund raising to a series of questions and answers and a lively but disastrous dialogue. Squelch that first question gently. Tell the guests that as soon as the business part of the meeting is over, there will be plenty of time to ask anything they want to know about. But right now is the time to finish what we are here for.

A parlor meeting can be held in a private club or in a private dining room at a hotel or restaurant. They're not as good as a home. They lack intimacy and warmth. Have parlor meetings there anyway if your host demands it. *Any* parlor meeting is better than most other fund raising events.

PHONE SQUADS. Another self-explanatory method, but a good one in many campaigns. There are times when you can't see your prospects, or there are just too many, or the potential gifts are small. That's when the telephone is a blessing and a valuable fund raising tool.

I used a small phone squad with great effect for a college campaign several years ago. We had about a dozen major gift prospects from different parts of the country who had not been seen. The chairman and two members of the committee spent the better part of a Sunday at the office and we put through long-distance calls to the prospects. Instead of each asker making his own calls, they all took part in every call by talking to the prospects on extension phones. It was almost impossible for a donor in St. Louis to say no to three men calling him from campus.

Another time I had the phone company install twenty phones in a large conference room and twenty members of the committee were able to make five hundred calls in one day. There they were, all in the same room calling prospects who had gotten a letter telling them to expect the call. An informal competition began among the committee members to see who could make the most calls, who could get the most pledges, and who could raise the most money. We accomplished three things: Marginal prospects were reached, some for the first time, and many of them gave; the committee had a good time. And we raised money.

A phone squad is a good method when you come down toward the end of the campaign and there are many prospects left who haven't been talked to. An annual campaign, where people give modest amounts every year, can use a phone squad to good effect. It's much better than a letter to all the nonrenewed givers.

It's important for you to train the people who will make the calls. You might have a sheet with instructions for each of them. There should be a brief pitch about your project so your people don't mumble or get flustered. It could have answers to questions they may be asked. You could stage an imaginary phone call or two so your squad will have examples of what they might expect at the other end of the line.

I've found evening phone squads don't work as well as Saturday or Sunday ones. I'll caution you not to call anybody at home before 10 A.M. on a weekend, even though you know it already. And, since your squad will work through lunch, try to get more callers than phones so your squad members can eat a sandwich you cleverly provided while someone else uses their phone.

Test a phone squad by picking fifty prospects in your low to low-medium giving range. You can call them cold, although a note telling them to expect the call is usually better. Use the campaign office or persuade a committee member to let you use his if there are three or more phones available. It is important that phone-squad members see and hear each other. Don't let them work alone because you'll lose a great deal of the enthusiasm and excitement that is generated in a one-room squad.

QUID PRO QUO. As you know, it means "something for something"; literally, "this for that." In your campaign it could mean cooperating with another group if they'll cooperate with yours. Serving on another committee if their chairman will serve on yours. Giving to another cause if the prospect gives to yours. There's almost no way to escape some kind of quid pro quo once you are involved in a fund raising project. People will know who you are and what you're doing. Your name will be added to lists all over the city, and you will become a target for everything from magazine subscriptions to kitchen remodeling to charity.

So use the quid pro quo as a tactic of your own before it's used on you. *You* decide which group or individual or campaign you want to deal with. Eliminate the others; after all, you can't do everything. Decide whether you want to make the first advance or whether it would be better to wait until you are approached. If you are good at compromise (bargaining) you could arrange for surprise help for your campaign.

Want some examples? You volunteer your committee to work at the tables of the hospital flea market if the hospital will recruit five people for your committee. Or you'll serve on the Boys' Club committee if the Boys' Club chairman hosts a parlor meeting for your project when he is finished.

RAFFLES. A raffle is a terrible fund raising method, but many organizations use it, and I am sorry to say they do raise money. Why is it terrible? Because the raffle-ticket buyer usually has no idea where his dollar or two went or why. Because the buyer cannot be considered a prospect for next year. Because the sellers—your committee people—could probably use raffle-selling time more profitably any number of different ways.

A raffle makes sense as a means of raising a small amount of money to buy uniforms for the Little League team, for example. Or if the tickets are high priced, the prize was contributed, and the profit is great.

Some organizations use raffles as a spur to the askers. Every prospect the asker sees or every contribution he brings in earns tickets. In a campaign with many small contributors and many lukewarm askers, it can have a positive effect.

Remember to tell the raffle winner to declare his prize as taxable income. And remember to check with your police chief to find out if a raffle is legal in your community.

RALLIES. You're trying to prevent a city park from being turned into a parking lot. Rally. You're trying to raise money to send food and medicine to a disaster area. Rally. Like newspaper ads, rallies are for one-time or crisis conditions, but not for the usual, traditional, typical campaign. It's very hard to raise a great deal of money at a rally. Almost all of the contributions are in cash, which can be lost or stolen; you certainly can't give receipts, and you probably won't have a good way of knowing who came, so you lose potential prospects.

You will usually need local government permission to hold a rally. You will certainly need mass exposure in the media, which may be hard to get. You may need posters and handbills and flyers and mailings, and they cost money. Your best way to gather a large crowd is word of mouth. Dozens and dozens of people calling hundreds of their friends.

Still, a rally could help influence a decision maker when you have a grant application to a city, county, or state agency. And if your project is particularly timely, you could draw a large crowd.

On the chance you are going to schedule a rally, here are some tips: Arrange a location with ample toilet facilities; be sure you have at least one doctor, a handy telephone, and the number of an ambulance service and hospital; the local police may station men at your rally, but if they don't, you should arrange for ushers and others to handle the crowd; get professional help with your lighting and microphone systems; have a clear, precise agenda and a program that takes no more than ninety minutes.

But don't try it unless you absolutely must!

ROASTS (See also Dinners, Per-Plate, and Testimonials.) A roast can be great when done right, and to continue the pun, it can be terrible if it's overcooked. Of course, roasts are a kind of testimonial where you show somebody how much you think of him by praising him with insults. You do it at a lunch or dinner with as large an audience as you can get. Presumably, the funnier and more outlandish the insult, the better.

I don't recommend roasts. Too many things can go wrong. The roastmaster has to be very skilled or the program could turn into an embarrassment. The man being roasted may not have the sense of humor you thought he had. And not too many causes should try to raise money at a funny event. A college, perhaps. The Crippled Children's Society? Hardly!

If there is someone your group wants to roast at a fund raising event and he's agreeable, make it a straight testimonial instead. You'll be glad you did. So will he.

SLOGANS. Your campaign doesn't need one. If you think the slogan "The March of Dimes" was a great idea, talk to somebody on the staff of the National Foundation. It has taken years (they're still at it) to persuade people to give more than a dime for polio research and now birth-defect research.

A slogan is an unnecessary tactic that is often used as a crutch by people who don't want to or can't talk about their project intelligently. I know I'm treading on some toes, but that's too bad. Sure "Tippecanoe and Tyler too" helped William Henry Harrison get elected in 1840, and other slogans helped start wars, and I have a few of my own in this book. But don't waste your time trying to think up a glorious slogan because it won't add a dime to your campaign.

SPORTS EVENTS. Sports events are another ticket method. They are used most effectively by large service organizations. Tickets to golf tournaments, football games, movie star tennis tournaments can be sold to people who don't know very much about your project. You have to sell thousands of tickets before you break even and I don't recommend them unless you have people in your organization who will buy and sell enough tickets to make a profit. If you depend upon publicity and advertising to draw people to the box office, you are courting failure. People *may* come, but if they don't, you're stuck with costs that could bankrupt you.

SYMPOSIA. See Convocations.

TELETHONS. Ah! The electronic medium, television; what have you wrought? There is hardly an organization in America that wouldn't give its chairman's eyeteeth for the chance at a fund raising telethon. Eight or twelve or twenty-four hours of almost constant pitches. Millions of prospects being asked for money by movie stars. Pledges pouring in so fast the computers can't keep pace.

Don't try it. If you get one handed to you, refuse it. It

could become a gift horse that will carry you into places you can't get out of. Like debt. Any organization with enough money to pay for a telethon can find a dozen better ways to spend it and raise more money. (Yes, I know much of the costs of a telethon are donated.)

Educational television stations with their technical people and talent already on the payroll are the only ones who should consider telethons. No, I'm not forgetting the Muscular Dystrophy Association. Tell you what you do: Write a letter to the Executive Director, MDAA, 3561 East Sunrise Drive, Tucson, Arizona 85718. Tell about your project and ask for advice on how to go about staging a telethon, how much it costs, how long it takes to plan, and so on. Then tell me I'm wrong.

TESTIMONIALS. Testimonials are trite, hackneyed, usually dreary events nobody enjoys except, perhaps, the guest of honor. There are some people who have so many plaques and awards they need a librarian to keep track of them. I recommend testimonials highly. They raise money.

For a good fund raising testimonial you will need four things: (1) a guest of honor; (2) a list of prospects; (3) a fund raising tactic; (4) a goal.

You may have the perfect candidate to be guest of honor already in your group, on your board, or among your donors. If not, you will have to find one. He should have some connection with your cause. It's not essential, but it makes the testimonial a more valid event. You can honor any good citizen at any time on behalf of almost any cause just because he's a nice guy. But your guest of honor should have clout or you may not do too well financially. If you honor the banker, you may raise money from building contractors who borrow from him. But if you honor a building contractor, his competitors may not feel they have to participate, although his subcontractors might. (See Max Billig's story, Chapter 12.)

You recruit a guest of honor almost the same way you recruit a chairman. You go to see him. You tell him he's been chosen for his many fine qualities—he can hardly disagree—plus the enormous good he can do for your project by accepting the honor you want to bestow upon him. Of course you will want to invite all his business associates, his friends, the members of his clubs, his staff, and anybody else he can think of to share in the great event. That list plus any names that you and your committee can add is your prospect list.

The fund raising tactic can be chosen from among a per-plate dinner or lunch; open pledges (not usually advisable because your guest could be embarrassed if his friends don't give as much as he had hoped they would) or prepledges—all the prospects are seen in advance and asked to contribute in honor of your guest. The guest of honor must be told about and agree to the tactic.

The goal can be a very effective plus tactic for a testimonial. You might set a goal to furnish a hospital room at your project, or build a new wing. To pay for a one-year or four-year scholarship. You decide in advance and then ask your guest of honor for his consent. Your guest could decide to give you the difference between the amount you raise and your goal if he's rich enough.

More often than not, testimonials lose sight of the project; people attend and give money because of the guest, not the cause. On the other hand, you will probably get new donors you couldn't consider realistic prospects.

Testimonials don't have to be huge events. Test it if you want to at a small luncheon. Certainly the guest of honor will attract his own family and close personal friends. Your inner group fills up the room so your guest isn't embarrassed.

THRIFT SHOPS. A thrift shop is really a business, and like a business, is good only if it's open during regular hours and has a large volume of trade. A small thrift shop is hardly worth the effort, and a large one can be a continuous headache. I don't recommend them. If you're determined to open a thrift shop for your project, try a flea market first. The experience you gain will help you decide whether or not you want a permanent outlet. Then talk to one of the groups that has a thrift shop and bring your accountant to check their books if they'll allow it.

TOURS. Airlines, travel agencies, tourist bureaus, and some resorts will give you a pretty good discount if you guarantee a certain number of customers for a tour. You charge customers the list price and the discount is yours. Your customers—prospects—go someplace they might have gone to anyway, they go with a group they probably know rather than strangers, and your project makes some money. I don't recommend or condemn tours. If your goal is small, a tour could be an event to use. While you are on the tour, you might even persuade some of the tourists to make an outright contribution. Remember to line up your group in advance and get their deposit checks. In most cases, once you guarantee a tour to an agency or carrier, you go through with it or pay anyway.

UNDERWRITING. No, it has nothing to do with insurance. Underwriting is when someone gives you money in advance to pay for all or part of a fund raising event or campaign. It's a great fund raising tactic and you should try to use it whenever you can. Your underwriter will understand his gift will be multiplied many times when he gives you the money to raise money. If he underwrites a fund raising convocation, for example, you can give him added prestige by telling your guests about it in programs and announcements.

I've told you never to try a campaign hoping you'll pay for it with money you raise as you go along. I'll repeat it and suggest you try to get someone to underwrite it. You could promise the underwriter you'll pay him back when the campaign is over and hope he won't accept.

If you have a clear budget and a carefully planned campaign, some foundations will help you as underwriters when they might not make an outright grant to you for a program.

Of course, the most logical source for underwriters is your inner group. Try them first.

VICTORY PARTIES. The campaign is over and you've topped your goal. Everybody can relax and take it easy. Have a victory party. A victory party is almost essential if you're hoping to raise money again next year. Have one even though your building is finished and paid for. The roof may leak and you'll need people again to help raise money for repairs. Almost anything goes at a victory party. Give out awards and prizes and mementos to the whole committee—to anyone who did anything. Including paid staff. By all means invite your major givers, and if there aren't too many, invite *all* your givers. Keep the formal program short—this is no time for a long-winded speaker.

Your committee should invite potential askers who might be recruited for your next campaign. Invite your mayor and congressman. They'll come if there's a chance to meet voters and your project isn't too controversial.

But keep one thing in mind—have fun. It's your victory party and you deserve it.

WEEKENDS. A weekend retreat with your committee

members can be an excellent way to educate them about your project, build their enthusiasm, and prepare them for the campaign. You can saturate them with seminars and discussions, slide shows or a film or two about your project. They'll get to know each other better and feel more like a team. Of course, the weekend should not be all work, but don't let it deteriorate into an all-play event, either.

Plan the weekend agenda as carefully as you would an approach to a potential chairman. If your project has enough money to start with, you could consider inviting the committee members as guests. It might prove to be a good investment. Or split the costs of transportation, room, and food with them.

There are conference centers all over the country that will help you plan everything. They are run by professionals who have dealt with all kinds of groups, probably some like yours. Ask your local Chamber of Commerce for a list of conference centers near you.

A weekend convocation that includes fund raising is worth doing because you have your prospects at a place with few distractions. Invite foundation executives after you find the ones making grants to projects like yours. They won't think you are trying to bribe them.

Weekend events don't have to be big. A few people, your top leadership, spending time together to plan the strategies of your campaign can do more for you than a dozen meetings in town.

WILLS AND BEQUESTS (See also Intent, Letters of.) The largest philanthropic gifts ever made were set up in wills. Henry Ford established the Ford Foundation in his will. Few people give away as much money while they're alive as they do after they die; that's an observation, not an indictment. Last year, Americans left more than $6 billion to charities in their wills. Some organizations were literally saved by wills in the past few years.

A wills and bequests program should be part of your campaign if you are an organization with some history and a potential future. It has to be a separate program; don't let it interfere with your current campaign, but don't treat it like a stepchild, either.

Wills and bequests should have a separate chairman and committee. Perhaps a small brochure too, telling about your long-range plans and how they could be funded by a farsighted donor.

It's no secret that lawyers are important for your wills committee, for obvious reasons. Do you have lawyers in your inner group? Put them in charge. You don't? How about inviting a group of lawyers to learn about your project and perhaps use their influence with their clients? Keep in touch with them regularly and send them material and information about your organization. If you convince the lawyers of your value, they may suggest you as a beneficiary if their clients ask for recommendations.

Your inner group and your major donors and prospects are, once again, your best sources for wills and bequests. Treat the subject with the delicacy it deserves: it's not an item for your agenda under New Business.

Send each wills and bequests prospect a letter asking for a private meeting. When you meet, try to direct the conversation so your prospect brings up the matter of wills. Don't put your project in danger of losing a current giver by saying something offensive even though you thought it wouldn't be. Unless your prospect is a boor, he'll do his best to make things easier for you.

It isn't necessary to talk about the size of the bequest unless your prospect brings it up. If he does, great. If not, all you should try for is an agreement in principle—just as in letters of intent. Then ask your prospect if it would be all right for you to talk to his lawyer. And that's it.

Wills and bequests may take years to produce results that warrant the effort. But you owe it to your project's future.

XMAS CARDS. Some of the most beautiful Christmas cards I have ever seen were printed for charitable organizations and sold at a profit by their committees. Obviously the profit you make depends upon the number of cards you print and sell, how much you charge for them, and the size of the discount you get from the printer.

You've probably received a Christmas card that said a friend sent a contribution to the community hospital in lieu of a gift to you. It's a good tactic because your friend made a reasonably good contribution; he then felt good because he could tell you about it without appearing immodest; and you learned about a project your friend was interested in. And all in the true spirit of Christmas.

If you use the Christmas-card method for the first time, try it out small and don't worry about making too much money the first year. Your test will teach you about printing costs, preparation time, distribution problems, reactions from prospects, and your potential for next year.

If you're not sending out "in lieu of a gift" cards, be sure you print something about your project on the Christmas cards, if it's only your name and address.

YOUTH. Young people are neither method, event, nor tactic. They're a resource. Most large campaigns relegate young people to a minor role, hoping they'll stay interested in the project until they grow up. A fuss is made over them from time to time, but the youngsters are usually not allowed in where the action is. I think it's a mistake.

On one of the best telephone squads I ever watched, teenagers made the calls. They had been thoroughly trained, of course, but I never saw a group more dedicated, more sincere, as tireless, or more enthusiastic. I would have trusted them with any assignment for any campaign I ever counseled.

Bring young people into your inner group. Give them real responsibility, not something they'll know isn't important. Try one or two of your brightest youngsters as chairmen of an event. Let them solicit a few of your better prospects. With so much competition for askers, can you afford to ignore a resource as large and available as young people?

ZIP CODES. If your list of donors and prospects is big enough to be on a computer, program a printout by zip code. You may need a quick list of people in Westport, Connecticut (06880), because a board member is going there and might see a few of them.

Zip codes are important in a direct-mail campaign. You may want letters sent only to known high-income codes like 44120 (Shaker Heights, Ohio) or 10583 (Scarsdale, New York).

The World Almanac and Book of Facts has an alphabetical list with zip codes of every town in the United States with 2,500 people or more. *Bullinger's Postal and Shipper's Guide* (in your library) lists zip codes in numerical order, so if you know the zip you can find the town.

Large cities with many zip codes can leave you guessing about an address if you don't know the city. For example, Sunset Boulevard, Los Angeles 90046, is a business district, but Sunset Boulevard, Los Angeles 90024, is residential with homes that cost $500,000 and up—way up. Call the post office. They'll tell you how to get a book that lists zip codes by street and number. You may not know 11 Lurmont Terrace, San Francisco, but zip 94133 is Russian Hill, hardly a slum.

11

Less-Than-Perfect Leaders

Not everybody in your group is as dedicated as you are. I've been talking as though everybody always comes to a meeting, everybody works hard at the project and the fund raising, everybody takes assignments and completes them. We both know it isn't so.

One of the hardest things in fund raising is working with trustees, directors, and committees—your askers. There are all sorts of plaques, awards, and prizes you can give them and the victory party is the place to do it.

But how do you handle the day-to-day, meeting-to-meeting problems your people can cause? The unfinished assignment, the nonworking asker, the volunteer who throws a monkey wrench into the works just as you're getting started?

I'm sure you've dealt with enough people in your life to be able to recognize certain personality types quickly. People do fall into categories we see repeated again and again. Perhaps I can help you to identify some types that crop up in a fund raising campaign, so you'll know about them in advance. You may be able to head them off, change their ways, or learn to cope with them.

However, I don't want you to think I'm like the clergy-man who berates the people *in* church because attendance is small. The foibles and attitudes I describe belong to those who are on the side of the angels already; I'd just like to see them do better, and these broad-stroke portraits may help you help them.

George Abercrombie has been around traditional fund raising a long time and is bored with it. He'd rather work on something fresh. So he comes to meetings with two or three alternative gimmicks and hopes he can push one of them through. He really means well and it's hard to get upset with him. He hopes you forgot about last year's parachute jumping contest and his guarantee it couldn't miss raising bundles of money.

It won't do you any good to try to talk him out of his ideas, so here's one way you might handle him: If the gimmick isn't totally absurd, tell him how great you think it is. Tell him it will add a new dimension to your project and new contributors as well. But it will have to be separated from the regular campaign so you can measure the pluses. Would George agree to be his special gimmick chairman, find the financial backing for it, and build his own committee without enlisting inner-group members? If he accepts, the only thing you have to be careful of is that he doesn't go to your regular support group for money. He just might surprise you.

Ethan Berghoffer is convinced all the other members of the committee are old-fashioned. What the campaign needs is new ideas for a new era. He has read about systems analysis, executive development, motivational psychology, and behavior modification. He is bright and talks convincingly. You fall into his trap if you allow yourself to be drawn into a debate on methods. Don't do it. Instead, ask him, "Who asks whom for money?"

If he can give you a good answer to that question, keep listening to him. Maybe he really has something. But if he can't, tell him you're fascinated with his idea and would like to know more about it after the meeting. Don't ridicule him, obviously. He really means well and he'll be helpful once he catches on that his ideas may be good, but they won't work unless he knows who asks whom.

Lamont Cranston has the unfortunate habit of not showing up when you need him and reappearing when you least expect him. There's not much you can do about it. His family and business commitments make him unpredictable, so don't count on him. Give him things to do that won't interfere with your plans if left undone, but would be an extra if he did them. Example: You may have people you really aren't counting on for gifts this year. Give their cards to Cranston—you have nothing to lose. But don't schedule him as the man to pick up your guest speaker at the airport!

Franklin DeMille is a hard-working committee member who prefers to work behind the scenes. He thinks of himself as an essential part of your project who maneuvers cleverly, cloak-and-dagger style, while others take the bows. Actually, he's terrified of confrontations and the spotlight and would do anything to avoid them. He'll never ask anybody for money, so don't waste your time hoping he'll change. Don't get into arguments with him at meetings; you'll just disrupt your meeting and lose the argument anyway. Instead, take advantage of him. Put him in charge of working with the printer or doing the research on foundations. Give him necessary but hidden assignments. Let him draw up the campaign calendar and see to it that everything is followed correctly; have him make all the follow-up calls to your committee; let him see to all the details of your special events. He'll free you for more important fund raising chores.

Lemuel Evans is president of the power company and the bank, chairman of the school board, president of the Boy Scouts, honorary chairman of the United Fund, member of two governor's commissions, and chairman of the greens commitee at the country club. He's Mr. Everything. His picture is in the paper more often than the mayor's, and you wonder how in the world he found time to go to Europe twice last year or testify at the hearings in Washington.

It's easy. He has an executive secretary who does everything including buying his ties and a young assistant who writes his speeches, goes to meetings as his proxy, and picks out the lawnmowers for the country club.

You may think your worries are over when Lemuel Evans agrees to be your chairman or becomes a member of your committee (he'll probably take the chairmanship and refuse a lesser role). But think twice! When you get Evans you really get the assistant, so check with the assistant first. Since he acts with Evans's authority, he *can* do great things for you unless he's swamped with other assignments. You can expect Lemuel Evans to show up at the kickoff and victory party, but the assistant is really your man, the one you'll deal with day to day. If *he* likes your project, you've got a winner.

Jeremy Fingerlake can point out every rich prospect within a radius of five hundred miles. He will regale you with stories and personal information about each of them. He knows them all, and you're delighted that Jeremy is on your committee. There's one small catch: He can give you a zillion reasons why he can't or won't ask them for money. From experience I can tell you you're wasting your time if you think you can get Jeremy to approach his wealthy contacts. Instead, turn Jeremy into your campaign mastermind. Spend as much time as you can with him and let him figure out the best possible approach to each prospect he knows. He'll know who knows whom and how to get from one to the other. Jeremy will delight in his role and figure out ways to get things done that will amaze you.

Make him your resources chairman and you'll be happy you did.

Gus Gillenwater is convinced nothing can succeed and he'll give you a dozen reasons to back it up. The world is shrouded in gloom and Gus is its prophet. He's sure there will be ice on the road the night of your big dinner and nobody will be able to get out of their garage; everybody is going to the football game and will be too tired to come to your auction that same night. Gus has so much fun being pessimistic and gloomy, he rarely comes up with any positive suggestions of his own. You will have to do it for him. Plant an idea with him that you need approved by the committee. Even though he doesn't bring it up himself, *you* bring it up as a brilliant idea that Gus gave you. Gus will work like a mule to make the idea succeed and he'll see to it that everybody else works, too.

Elliot Harmony is a master at compromise and every committee has at least one. He can't stand conflict, and when there are differences of opinion he always tries to find a middle ground. He is great to have around because he often finds ways out of your dilemma. On the other hand, he may find a middle ground that is really quick-sand—your campaign could sink out of sight. You will be able to recognize Elliot Harmony easily enough, but dealing with his fatal compromise may not be so easy. When you're sure he is leading you into the swamp, fight back. Oppose his compromise with vigor; he may withdraw it if he thinks he is making you angry. Don't crush him, he's really eager to help. If there's still some doubt about the compromise, appoint a committee to study it and keep Elliot from serving on it—get on the committee yourself, if you can. Elliot won't mind. Study committees are a form of compromise and that's all he really wants.

Vernon Ingersoll comes to every meeting with a batch of clippings about every other campaign in the state. He'll ask why you can't get more exposure and he'll ask his questions in the middle of other important discussions. Logic won't work with Vernon, so don't argue with him that your project may not be important enough to make the cover of *Newsweek*. Vernon is really dedicated to your campaign and he feels frustrated that the whole community isn't clamoring to take part in it. If you can neutralize him you'll have a hard-working committee member. So make him chairman of the Publicity Committee in addition to his other assignments. Talk to a few other members of your group in advance, so when you nominate Vernon the vote will be unanimous and he won't be able to refuse.

Norman Jackson is a thoughtful, intelligent board member who knows more about prisons than anybody else on your prison-reform committee. He's written a book on the subject and is respected by everyone who knows anything about it. He's essential to your project—you know it and he knows it. And he may be the most difficult board member you may have to deal with if he decides he doesn't want to take part in fund raising. I wish I had a clever trick or a glib paragraph you could use to change his mind, because he could be a great asker. I don't. The only suggestion I have is this: Be your most persuasive self when you ask him to work on fund raising. Try any and every argument you have. When he insists he won't be an asker, compromise and tell him you need him as a spokesman and use him as the speaker for your fund raising event. He will probably agree so long as he doesn't have to ask for money.

If your Norman Jackson won't ask for money and *isn't* an expert in your field, you're stuck with an unproductive board member and you should be aware of it.

★   ★   ★

From George Abercrombie to Norman Jackson, I have given you thumbnail caricatures of ten prevalent less-than-perfect leaders. There are others, like Abel Kingsford, who boasts abut his dependability but has a short memory; Charles Llewellyn, who always knows a better way of doing things just as you've finished all your planning; and Howard Meredith, who insists he's on the team but is still thinking about his own gift three months after the campaign is over.

Or Marlowe Newsome, who wants your church group to do something about air pollution while you're having trouble buying furniture for the Sunday school, and Justin Oberlin, who would postpone everything until the time is right.

You know them as well as I do—maybe better, because they're on your committee. Each will have to be treated differently and you are responsible for figuring out how to do it. It's crucial to your campaign because you need them and you need them working together toward a common goal. Don't treat everybody alike and don't ignore their differences because you're too wrapped up in your project.

If you rely on the notion that everything will turn out right because your inner group will do the right things without guidance, you're making a mistake. Human nature will do you in and you'll be spending more time than you should trying to correct mistakes that could have been avoided.

Draw up a profile of each member of your inner group. In private, ask each one about the others. Find out which ones they like and don't like and why. Study them until you know them as well as is possible under your circumstances. Then devise strategies for each one that will ensure cooperation among them and will get the most out of all of them.

The baseball manager who knows the most about baseball doesn't always win; the manager who gets the most out of his players usually does.

If you recognized a negative trait of your own among the ones I described, get rid of it and don't feel bad. Psychologists will tell you the habits we dislike in others are ones we recognize as our own.

And one thing more: Remember that everybody in your inner group is wonderful. Who else would give up Monday-night football on television to come to a planning meeting? Who else would be willing to do the menial, unappreciated things you ask of them? Nice people, that's who. So cuddle them and love them, because they deserve it.

12

Use Your Imagination

I'm not a psychologist and this is not a book about how the mind works. But ideas and imagination can make a difference in your campaign—maybe a critical difference.

The great psychologist William James said, "Genius, in truth, means little more than the faculty of perceiving in an unhabitual way." If you do what everybody else does and it's well planned and organized, you will probably wind up all right. But is that all you want? Doesn't your project deserve a little bit more than everybody else's? Isn't there something you can do to lift your campaign one notch higher?

Let me give you an example of what I mean. A friend of mine was working with a group that was interested in prison reform. In addition to being a fine writer, he ran a famous cooking school in his city. Part of the plan for the prison-reform campaign called for a luncheon of wealthy prospects to educate them about the project, and the luncheon was scheduled at the cooking school.

Prospects arrived expecting a gourmet meal and some interesting talk. This would be much better than the restaurant lunch or hotel food they were usually subjected to when they were pitched. But my friend, already one notch above other campaigns, took it still another notch higher. The day before the luncheon he visited the local prison and talked to the cook. Then he served his guests exactly what the prisoners were eating for lunch. It had a profound effect upon the guests. Short of locking them up for the night, he couldn't have given them a better way of understanding why his project was important.

Here's another example: A group of ladies in a wealthy suburb had an annual event to raise money for the local hospital. Because the suburb was so very wealthy, the residents were the targets of countless appeals. The hospital ladies began to worry whether or not their invitations to the annual event would be opened, let alone answered. So they found and rented a stately carriage—the kind you see in movies about Louis XIV. They persuaded some of their husbands to serve as coachmen and footmen, and they dressed them in appropriate costumes. Drawn by four immaculately white horses (rented), the carriage made its way slowly through the streets while footmen hand-delivered the invitations on silver salvers. Corny? Gimmicky? Perhaps, but it worked. In fact, some of the residents were a little peeved because the carriage *didn't* stop at their houses.

You realize, of course, that I'm not suggesting you have invitations to a prison meal delivered by carriage. I'm asking you to have some fun and use your great gift of imagination.

Be outrageous. Let your imagination come up with ridiculous ideas. Don't stop yourself when you start to imagine holding your next meeting on the moon. It may be the beginning of something that includes an astronaut, and it fits your campaign. Don't cheat your campaign of a gift only you can make: the use of *your* brain.

Just recently I asked an associate to let his imagination loose for ideas for one of our clients, and see what happened. It was fun. We laughed a great deal at some wonderfully zany notions he came up with. He talked about the Queen of England and whether we could get her to make a pitch . . . or maybe the Emperor of Japan. The more we laughed, the wilder the ideas became. We were laughing until our sides ached and then one of the ideas didn't look so crazy after all. How about Prince Bernhard of The Netherlands? Well, maybe not as a pitchman, but would he bring greetings to our group if we planned something in his country? With a bit of toning down, a snip here, some padding there, we had a perfect way to kick off our campaign, a convocation in The Hague for an international project. We're still laughing about it.

Sometimes thinking about a problem helps you chop away the clutter so you can see what you are really looking for. Example: Some years ago I was working on a campaign that I was sure would interest Adlai Stevenson, and if he took part in the project it was bound to succeed. As one of the most famous men in the world, he was bombarded daily with demands on his time and energy. We had nobody in our inner group who knew him and we couldn't think of a clever idea to get his attention. We thought about and eliminated dozens and dozens of possibilities until we were exhausted. The next day I picked up the phone and called him at his Chicago law office. Five minutes with his secretary and she put him on. He said yes.

Not long after I started working in fund raising, I committed a horrible blunder. I scheduled the annual $50-a-plate end-of-the-campaign dinner-dance on Mother's Day ($50 was a lot of money in those days). We didn't discover the conflict in dates until everything was printed and all the arrangements were made. We couldn't change anything. I was terrified. There was no way out—the only thing my mind would focus upon was where would I get another job? But then, in ways I cannot explain, and without any conscious effort on my part, my brain worked on the problem and the conditions as it saw them.

Solution: A letter to all the men on our invitation list *reminding* them the annual dinner was on Mother's Day (some, I found out later, had forgotten). The letter suggested it might be a nice way to spend an evening with their wives—bring the kids—and contribute to a worthy project at the same time.

It worked or I might still be looking for a job. It worked because it was logical and it fitted the problem. My unconscious solved it for me, just as yours can solve problems for you if you give it a chance.

There are times when just staring out the window will do it. As it did once for my dear friend Max Billig, a fund raising genius who died a few years ago. For reasons of his own, Max would disappear from time to time, come back, and get another job. One day he found himself the development director for an old, tired hospital in New York. His board wouldn't do a thing, the doctors wouldn't help, staff was paralyzed. . . . So Max sat in his office staring out the window at the river. He looked at the same view that each of the former development directors had looked at, but somehow Max saw the river differently. He got up, put on his coat, and left. He went down to the waterfront and into the office of the harbormaster. He took the harbormaster to lunch, cocktails, and dinner. For two days Max wined and dined the harbormaster until the harbormaster agreed to serve on the board of Max's hospital. Then Max explained that every board member was inducted at a dinner—a testimonial dinner. The harbormaster was going to be guest of honor and Max made all the arrangements.

When you understand that with a wave of his hand, a harbormaster can keep a boat from docking until the cargo becomes obsolete, you then understand that everybody had to come to the dinner at $1,000 a table. Ship owners, warehouse owners, truckers, labor unions, everybody came—2,000 of them. It was a smash! Three days later Max disappeared again.

Here's another example of how the conditions of a problem helped to solve it. We had scheduled a major dinner and we had more than eight hundred reservations. The guest speaker was the ambassador from a foreign country to the United States. We were prepared to make a pitch for funds immediately after the ambassador finished his speech. From experience we knew that many people would leave right after he spoke so they could avoid the crush at the exit and at the parking lot. But if many of them left immediately after the ambassador spoke, the disturbance would ruin the pitch.

It was a sticky problem. We couldn't put armed guards at the door to make sure nobody went home before the fund raising; we couldn't do any fund raising before the inspirational speech we were expecting from the ambassador; and we didn't want to lose the drama of the event and hope that people would respond later on.

Here's what we did: We stationed guards at all the exits and gave them specific instructions *not* to prevent anybody from leaving. They were to stand there. When the evening began, the chairman asked everybody to remain seated until the ambassador and the ambassador's wife left. The chairman hinted that anyone who left would be rude, and the guards at the door suggested there could possibly be a security reason for asking them to remain seated. They stayed.

Before we leave the subject of imagination, it's important to see the difference between inspiration and gimmickry. It's easy. An inspiration keeps your objective in constant view—financial results. A gimmick doesn't.

Here's an example: Not too long ago, a San Francisco

committee that ran an annual dinner-dance that was a social, slam-bang fund raising bash hired a local publicity man. His most recent success had been to let loose a hundred doves from the Golden Gate Bridge to publicize the arrival of a cruise ship on its maiden voyage. One hundred white doves soaring around the ship and the bridge made an exquisite picture in all the papers and TV news shows.

Unfortunately, the publicity man got his needle stuck on doves. He told the committee that at the height of the evening, from the spotlight room high above the ballroom, he would free a hundred doves. They would swoop and soar around the room as the guests were dancing, and it would be unique and lovely. One of the committee members reminded him that doves, after all, were pigeons, and pigeons are noted for their bad manners. The answer to the bad manners was Scotch tape. The committee agreed.

At the appointed hour, a hundred pigeons swooped to the ceiling of the ballroom, and finding no way out, swooped down to the floor, where they pecked desperately at their Scotch-tape diapers. Chaos! End of gala evening.

So stare out the window, use your imagination, but remember the doves.

13

A Few More Q's and A's

Over the years I have collected two kinds of questions about fund raising: the ones I'm asked most often and the ones I ask people who come to me for advice. Some questions don't fit into neat categories, but they can't be ignored. So here are a few more Q's and A's.

Do you have tax deductibility?

A second part to that question is: Are you a properly registered corporation with officers, directors, bylaws? If you are, fine. If not, I won't bore you with the Internal Revenue Service definitions of who can claim tax deductibility, but I will give you a piece of simple advice: Talk to a lawyer. This may sound elementary to you, but you would be astonished at the number of people who get into trouble with their income-tax returns because they thought they were giving away tax-deductible money and weren't. If you have already filed and received your letter from Internal Revenue, double check to see if you are listed in the *Cumulative List of Organizations* published by the Treasury Department. Your library probably has a copy, or you can call the local office of the Internal Revenue Service listed in your phone book.

If you are a publicly supported charitable organization

(Section 501 [c] [3] of the Internal Revenue Code), your contributors may take a deduction of up to 50 percent. But that's the law as of the time I'm writing this book. Things change. Check everything concerning taxes with your accountant and your attorney. You will find you have to file a Form 990, which will include, among other things, a statement of your income and your expenditures. You will also have to report any salaries you paid to officers, directors, trustees, and employees.

Are you planning to influence legislation with the money you raise?

If you are, you can't get tax deductibility, but that does not have to be fatal to your plans. If your objectives have enough appeal to enough people, you can still raise money although the gifts may be smaller than they would have been under deductible circumstances. You may still get tax deductibility for *some* of your contributions anyway. If part of your project calls for educating people about the conditions you are trying to change through legislation, you can set up a tax-deductible organization for the educational side of your program. But not for lobbying.

Should you channel funds through an existing organization?

You don't understand the question? If yours is a new project that is vital, timely, and can't wait until you become incorporated and tax deductible, you can still raise money and give your contributors a tax deduction. Find a funnel—a church, a service organization with IRS clearance, an existing foundation—and talk to them. Ask them if they will accept contributions that you will solicit and then earmark the money for your project. Don't worry, you won't be breaking the law. The funnel organization won't let you; they'll check you out with their own attorneys first because you'll insist on it. By not waiting for your own IRS application to clear, you may be able to take advantage of a particular event or favorable circumstances that focus attention on your project and make fund raising a little easier.

Using a funnel organization is a good device for a one-shot campaign. It will save you money—you won't have to incorporate or file with the IRS—and it might keep you from perpetuating yourself once your project is finished.

It's not a bad idea for you even if you're going to file on your own and keep going. The funnel group may like your project well enough to join with you when you go out on your own.

Two things to remember about using a funnel: (1) They will probably want some money from you to cover their costs. That's fair. But if they want more than 10 percent, look someplace else. (2) The funnel organization should have some bearing upon your project. You don't have to be identical to them, but if your objectives are too far apart, the IRS may not like it.

Are there local or state laws you must obey?

Dozens of cities and twenty-three states plus the District of Columbia have passed laws that affect fund raising. Some of them could stop you cold in your tracks if your costs of raising money are higher than they allow. Penalties for breaking the laws vary, but they include stiff fines, possible jail terms, and the kind of publicity you don't want or need. Some regulations require complex forms to be filled out, reports that must be sent back by an established deadline, or licenses. Check out the possible legal restrictions in your community. The chief of police or your local district attorney are easy to find and they'll be happy to send you any material that will have a bearing on fund raising. Then contact the attorney general or the secretary of state in your state. They'll let you know about statewide laws. Your local librarian will tell you who they are and where to reach them.

Should you join forces with the local Community Chest or United Fund?

In many communities there is an annual battle between some of the national health campaigns and local United Funds. The major health campaigns feel they can raise more money on their own than they can by joining the United Fund. United Funds argue they cut down the number of appeals to their community and cut fund raising costs at the same time. They're both right.

If there's a chance your project might fit into the United Fund in your community, call the chairman and talk to him. Find out if you do fit and how much money he thinks you could get by snuggling under his umbrella. He'll ask you who your committee members are and whether they'll work for him. Each of you will be trying to figure out if joining forces pays, and the negotiations could take quite a while.

Here's what you should be thinking about: Would you object if your project became part of another group and lost some of its identity? Can you raise substantially more money on your own? Would you be prepared to deal with a community conflict. Would your committee go along with your decision? Would the United Fund allow you to have a supplemental campaign if you joined it?

Remember, not everybody gives to the United Fund. You may have prospects on your list that only you can reach. So I don't have a direct answer to the question, but you do. Consider carefully before you decide.

Has the one source of most of your money stopped, or is it about to stop?

It's easy to become the beneficiary *and* the victim of a

single source of money. It's so easy it happens all the time. Talk to anyone on the staff of the Ford Foundation and he'll tell you how fearful they are that some of their beneficiaries won't believe them when the grants come to an end.

It's a trap to be wary of, because while the money is coming in and you're involved in your program and you're spending it to do good things, you don't want to spoil your day with thoughts about raising money. So now you're stuck. What do you do?

You won't like the answer any more than the fat person likes the doctor's diet when he's hoping for a pill to make him skinny overnight. What you do is start over from the beginning, and if you're lucky you'll have enough money left from your primary source to finance a good campaign.

In desperation you might go back to your primary source and ask if they might help you find another primary source. It won't work. Even if it did, sooner or later you're going to have to start over the right way, and you'd better do it while you have enough time and money.

What about deferred gifts, trusts, and such?

You should think about deferred giving if:

- your project is going to be around for a long time, like a hospital or university, and/or

- your current income is adequate, and/or

- you have several prospects who won't or can't make major gifts any other way, and/or

- you have a dedicated tax lawyer and accountant on your payroll or your committee, and/or

- you have an advisory group skilled in investments to manage the deferred gifts, and/or

- you have enough askers who know about deferred giving.

Here are just a few types of deferred gifts:

Charitable remainder annuity trust
Charitable remainder unitrust
Charitable income (lead) trust
Charitable gift annuity
Pooled income fund trust—life income contract
Revocable charitable remainder trust
Totten trust
Gift of personal residence or farm with retained life estate

They are as complicated as they sound. You have to consider the age of the donor, his family, his tax bracket, the tax bracket he is likely to be in later on, the dollar value of his estate today and what it might be when he dies, and so on almost to infinity.

I recently attended a seminar by one of the country's leading tax lawyers. I came away with a seven-pound volume of statistical tables, tax form specimens, restrictions, agreements, and government regulations about the deferred giving types on my list. I also came away with this understanding: No two people are in the same position when it comes to a deferred gift. They will have to talk to their accountants and their lawyers no matter what they tell you they want to do.

So if you have a prospect for a deferred gift, get him to agree *in principle* that he wants to do something for your project while he's still alive, or he wants your project to benefit after he's gone. Then arrange a date to sit down with his lawyer—bring your lawyer too—and draw up the agreement. Chances are his lawyer will use a method with the best tax break. If the method his lawyer chooses doesn't sit right with the needs of your project, tell him. But don't fight too hard. He's trying to do right by his client and he could wreck the deal.

What kind of prospect and donor records do you have?

If you have more than three thousand names on your list, you should look into the possibility of a punch-card system so you can find what you want quickly. For many more names you may need a computer; you'll certainly need at least one full-time person working on your list to keep it up to date.

More important than the system is the information you are keeping on each giver. Here's what you should try to get:

Home address and phone number
Wife's name
Business address and phone number
Type of business
Committee member
Gift rating
Amount and date of pledge or gift
Name of asker
Terms of pledge or gift (when and how to be paid or whether it has sponsored a scholarship or hospital bed)
Next billing date
Next soliciting date
Special notes: ("Don't phone after 5 p.m."; "All correspondence to his office address.")

You could add his club memberships, his other charitable interests, the schools he attended, his hobbies and other personal data that are important.

For prospects, the special notes are very important.

That's where you put "His attorney is J. Smith—takes Smith's advice"; "Charlie Green will see him June 24."

You can put the information on cards (at least 5″ by 8″) or on sheets to be put in a binder if you have only a few hundred names; it's not that important so long as you know what you need to know about your prospects and donors. Don't worry about putting the information on a computer, unless you have at least 3,000 names and addresses.

What about those family foundations—how do you deal with them?

Some wealthy people set up their own foundations and run them personally. Treat the family foundation the same way you would any top prospect—as an individual. If the family foundation has a consultant, you'll find out as soon as you make your first contact. Then treat the consultant as an individual. Don't let the word "foundation" confuse you when you are really dealing with one individual.

Should you add corporations to your list of prospects?

I suppose so, if you have a chairman or committee member with extraordinary clout. But corporations give away about 5 percent of the money raised for charitable causes, so don't be surprised if you're turned down or get much, much less than you hoped for.

The reasons you'll get from the corporation will include these: They're extremely visible, so everybody goes after them (Corporations are so highly visible that they are bombarded by requests for contributions. The contributions executive of a major corporation recently reported that he was receiving proposals for funds at the rate of one every 23 seconds!); they give only in those communities where they have offices or factories; they have to be careful not to antagonize certain stockholders who don't believe in what you are doing; they give only to the arts or they give to everything except the arts.

There are many notable exceptions among corporations, of course. In some cases philanthropy is a basic part of corporate policy. Often there is a corporation committee whose job it is to evaluate proposals and decide which ones to support.

If you have a list of corporate prospects, here's what you do: Write to the head of public affairs or the public relations department. Ask for a copy of their giving guidelines and a list of their previous year's donations. You'll probably get them. Then treat the corporation just like a foundation.

Some large corporations have their own foundations with professional staffs in charge. Treat them as you would any other foundation, although you will find corporate foundations usually have narrower giving guidelines—they'll give only to education or never to education, only in the northeast or northwest.

Of course, if your chairman knows the chairman of the corporation, forget what I just told you. Lunch between your man and their's will tell you all you need to know and will probably start the ball rolling.

What do you know about professional fund raisers in case you need one?

Professionals in fund raising are involved in billions of dollars every year, but they don't have to be licensed. Two national professional fund raisers' organizations are the American Association of Fund-Raising Counsel and the National Society of Fund Raising Executives—and neither one has very high standards for membership. They require five years' experience but that experience could be as third assistant at the United Fund of Moose Jaw, Saskatchewan.

As in most professions, fund raising has its fools and geniuses, journeymen and experts, pedestrians and thinkers. Unfortunately, you may not be able to tell which is which when you need one, so here are some suggestions on the kind of person to look for:

Someone with a love of language and the ability to handle English gracefully. Much of fund raising is communications.

Someone who is a problem solver, with a relish for puzzles and challenges.

Someone with a wide range of information who knows how to tell you what he knows. He'll have to learn your project and tell others about it.

Someone who really likes people and gets that feeling across to you without the need to say it.

And here's what you should and should not expect from a good professional:

The good professional

Will tell you your strengths and your weaknesses.
Will help you evaluate and rate your inner group.
Will create a master plan for you that fits your project.
Will help you make your strongest case.
Will help you find your prospects.
Will write material you can't write yourself.
Will train you and your inner group to be effective askers.
Will help you make appeals to the right foundations.
Will help you establish your goal.
Will help you choose the right events and plan them.
Will help you set up record systems that are right for you.
Will coordinate publicity if you need it.
Will help you get started on the right foot, stay with you

as long as you need him, and guide you from time to time afterward.

Will charge you a flat fee or salary you agree upon in advance.

Won't ask your prospects for money.

Won't have special privileges with foundations.

Won't have a list of prospects for your campaign in his hip pocket.

Won't work on commission.

Won't guarantee results.

A few years ago the *Wall Street Journal* had an article about a professional fund raiser. They pictured him as a hot-shot, fastest-gun-in-the-West type. He popped off about his current campaign, how he faced down reluctant donors. Then he drove off into the sunset, riding his trusty ancient-vintage foreign car. He had even given the car a cutesy name, the kind you give to a horse, and it completed the image of the restless hero who rides into town, cleans up the bad guys, and leaves an adoring, goggle-eyed community behind him.

Stuff and nonsense.

Get rid of *any* professional who would like you to think he's the Lone Ranger.

If you're still not sure about whether you need a professional or which one to hire, this is what you ought to do: Write to the President of the National Society of Fund Raising Executives, 1101 King Street, Suite 3000, Alexandria, Virginia 22314. Tell her your problem. If she thinks you need professional help, ask for her recommendation. Then pay a fee to whomever she recommends to find the right person for you. Before you hire *anyone*, be sure he can do what I told you a good professional should be able to do.

Could you learn about fund raising by attending seminars, so you won't have to hire a professional?

Within recent years a phenomenon has sprung up in the fund raising business: the seminar. Some of them guarantee to turn anybody into a professional overnight. One brochure I saw promised to cover every imaginable fund raising problem and technique in one day—from 9 A.M. to 4:15 P.M., with time out for lunch and "ample time allocated to questions and answers." And all for $30, which included the cost of a certificate of graduation.

Another one listed the keynote address as "Synergism for the Decade: Optimizing the Fund-Raising Public Relations Interface." (I should have attended because I still don't know what it means.)

Still others promise to teach you "grantsmanship," or how to rip off a foundation or government agency.

Because many of my ethical colleagues know we have a lot to learn from each other, we do have seminars from time to time in various cities. But they're for experienced pros who want to know a little more about things like computers or the intricacies of trusts. No seminar will turn you into a professional, so save your money. But several campaigns for your project will teach you what *you* need to know.

14

Foundations: Some Myths and Facts About the Money Tree

It has become fashionable nowadays to take potshots at foundations; they make wonderful targets. They're rich and visible, and some of the giants were founded by so-called robber barons. Because of several recent books and congressional hearings, the foundation image has become tarnished, and it's tough for them to fight back without making things worse. They don't need me to defend them, but it would be useful to look at foundations and see them as they are—a peculiar American institution trying to do good things, sometimes succeeding, sometimes not.

There is a foundation mythology and everybody who deals with foundations has his pet myth. I've collected a number of them, because your approach to foundations will be based upon the way you feel about them, and the way you feel about them will be based upon your own mythology.

MYTH: *Foundations give away most of the charitable money in the United States.*

Foundations give away about 5 percent of the philanthropy dollar. So if you are thinking that all you need for your campaign is foundation money, think again. You're still going to need an organized effort.

If foundations don't give away most of the money, why all this fuss about them? Because foundations have the capacity to make big gifts and it's worth the time and effort to go after a major gift prospect. Because foundations set trends in philanthropy. A foundation gift can give you instant credibility—people will assume you are what you say you are because a foundation has checked you out. Because some institutions depend upon foundations for up to 50 percent of their budget. And because you are going to go after them anyway.

MYTH: *Foundations are fortresses that cannot be taken by direct assault; only a sly approach can work.*

Foundations are in the business of giving money away, and giving away large sums of money intelligently can be agonizing. For a time I was consultant to a foundation that gave away $1 million a year, and it wasn't fun making decisions that could mean life or death to a worthwhile project. But since we had to give the money away, we appreciated a direct approach. Big foundations appreciate it too. Nobody likes to be sneaked up on.

MYTH: *If one major foundation supports you, they all will; or if one major foundation supports you, the others won't.*

It may help to have a grant from a giant with a large research staff. The big one checks you out and, in a sense, puts a stamp of approval on your project. And foundations often work together; one director may sometimes call another for help in funding a project he likes. On the other hand, a small foundation may look for projects where they can make a substantial impact, and won't support you if you are getting a bundle from a giant. But there are no rules, there is no collusion, and there is no competition. If you believe this myth, you could shut yourself off from possible help or delude yourself into thinking you've found a key to the mint.

MYTH: *If you are brand-new, foundations won't give you anything. Only proven organizations need apply. Foundations always play safe. An innovative project won't stand a chance.*

If by playing safe you mean foundations check out their applicants, you're right. They're not in the habit of flinging money around just because they have a lot of it.

Foundations are constantly looking for new and creative projects. They *need* applications for the same reason a store needs customers; it's their business. Without applications from us they would have no reason to exist. Don't sell your new project short. If it's really good, no matter how original or strange or offbeat, there's a chance you will find a foundation that will help you.

MYTH: *Foundation executives are stodgy, clubby types who care only about the Harvards and other "establishment" causes.*

Sarah Pinkham (not her real name) is a young, attractive woman who was senior officer of one of the foundation giants. She had a secretary but she answered her own phone most of the time. She became interested in a new project that had applied for a grant and she called me. Among other things, she wanted me to work with the group, help them find other sources of funding, and see whether they were too "establishment." She didn't want to support something that helped only a few people when she could approve grants to help many.

Esau Provence (not his real name) is an executive of another foundation giant. He's a young intellectual and speaks with a charming Caribbean accent. For several years now he has been scouring the South looking for ways to help poor kids get a better education than their parents had. He practically lives out of a suitcase, traveling from one obscure town to another, when he could, if he chose to, stay in his comfortable New York office.

Lastly, three mature ladies I'll call Mrs. Redd, Mrs. Whyte, and Mrs. Blu—directors of a modest foundation— are educated ladies, all-American ladies who look as though they have spent their lives well protected and well provided for. During an hour-long conversation they asked clear, intelligent questions about a project I had brought to them. Then they practically wrote the application for me and told me how much to ask for. It was a sizable amount for a health program in the rural South.

MYTH: *If you don't know somebody personally at a foundation, you'll never get a dime. Or if you* do *know somebody, you're a cinch.*

It never does any harm to know somebody on a foundation board or staff. It entitles you to one free phone call on behalf of your project. After that you'd better have a legitimate application. But if you don't know anybody at a foundation, you're still entitled to a letter followed by a phone call.

If a foundation executive knows you and trusts you, he'll tell you right out what your chances are of being funded so you won't have to wait around. He'll also tell you about any changes in his foundation's policy so you won't waste your time applying for a health grant just as they switch to the arts. And since foundation executives talk to each other all the time, you could find out the Zilch Foundation would be a logical place for you to apply now.

Having friends is nice, and having foundation friends is nice too. But your project better be a good one. If it is *and* you know somebody, you're in fine shape.

MYTH: *Foundations love to say no.*

They hate it. They hate it so much they have exhausted dictionaries trying to find different ways to say it, because even the richest foundation turns down hundreds of applications for each one it approves. There's no fun in telling somebody you won't help him. One of my gripes with some foundations is that they don't say no clearly enough. By trying to be gentle they sometimes confuse the applicant. A classic example is a former client. Their woman in charge of foundation appeals showed me the neatest, most complete file of letters I had ever seen. She told me it was her "active" file—each letter held out a promise of future support from a foundation. I was delighted until I started to read them. Every letter said no, but was couched in language an anxious reader might interpret as maybe. I didn't have the heart to destroy her illusion. Time and the absence of grants did it for me.

MYTH: *Foundations deliberately try to discourage appeals by making impossible demands upon applicants.*

Some foundations do have forms you have to fill out and some of the forms make an income-tax return look simple. But let me assure you it will help your legitimate project because it weeds out others that aren't as worthwhile as yours. If you get to the point where a foundation asks you to fill out one of its forms, you may have reached a second foundation plateau. Many foundations won't even send you a form to fill out unless they think you've got something.

Foundations will ask you to report on what you did with their money. They have to, because they could be in deep trouble if you used their money for illegal purposes or tried to influence an election, for example. I cannot imagine a legitimate organization getting upset because there was some paperwork involved before or after getting a foundation grant.

MYTH: *Writing a foundation application requires special training.*

Anybody who can write clear, understandable English can write a foundation proposal. Anybody.

MYTH: *There are experts you can hire who know the combination to the foundation vault.*

This is a myth perpetuated by the so-called experts themselves. They even hold seminars on their specialty and charge high fees. One such expert recently charged $8,000 for sending out one hundred form letters to foundations on his client's behalf. You can read and write English. You have intelligence and curiosity. You can be a foundation expert in a week, but not if you send out form letters.

And finally, the most erudite myth I have ever read, from *The House of Intellect* by Jacques Barzun.*

It says much for the acceptance of foundation folklore that we all know what a project is: It is something neatly clamped in a folder, not too thin and not too bulky, and typed preferably on an electric typewriter. The last page consists of figures, headed "Estimated Budget" and divided into three- or five-year slices. The project is in truth a literary form, like the Shakespearean sonnet, and its correct composition is an art not vouchsafed to everyone. . . . Each must follow style and fashion; the idea must be turned in such a way that it shall make the project different from all others, yet "in line with current programs" and at the same time "widely applicable" if successful.

Nobody would argue that Dr. Barzun's prose isn't lovely, if somewhat weighty. But his cynicism is not justified. To

*New York: Harper & Row, 1959, p. 183.

be blunt, he's wrong. A few days before I wrote the first edition of this book, one of my clients received $300,000 from a major foundation after a brief letter, two personal interviews, and a two-page application.

Okay, you're convinced. Now what do you do? The first thing to remember about foundations is that they are run by people—human beings like you and me. Some are brilliant, others are dull, some are gentle, others are strong, but all of them are human.

The second thing to do is to find the foundations that support projects like yours. You can find that out easily from *The Foundation Directory* in your library. You can contact the Foundation Center at 79 5th Avenue, New York, N.Y. 10003 (212) 620-4230. In addition, there are over 100 regional collections in cities throughout the United States. You can find out where the nearest one is to you by getting in touch with the Foundation Center. They will be happy to tell you where you can find out what you need to know about foundations and where the closest cooperating collection is located.

Records of foundations in your state are kept by the secretary of state in your capital city. Go there. Or you can send a postcard to any foundation and ask for a copy of its annual report. Then you'll see who they support and how much they give away so you won't ask for an impossibly large amount or so little you'll be ignored.

From your simple research you'll learn the name of the person to contact. Send him a letter describing your project (here's where the brief case statement pays off), how you fit into the purposes of his foundation, and why you want to meet with him. Be brief and readable. If you don't get an answer in about two weeks, call him.

Four things can happen: (1) You'll get turned down flat. (2) You'll be told something that means come back later. (3) You'll get a letter asking for more information. (4) You'll get an appointment.

If you get answer number 3 or 4, all the work you've done up to now with your board and committee and your lawyer and accountants becomes crucial. (You realize I'm always assuming you have a real case and can show how your project will do what you say it can do.)

Your budget and cost figures and the people in charge of your project will be checked out. Your sincerity is the only other thing you'll need. That and patience, because you may have to wait for the foundation board to meet before you get your grant. If you are successful and get a foundation grant, don't flaunt it. Because of foundation mythology, some of your prospects may think you're well taken care of and give their money elsewhere.

Once you have gone all the way through the routine of dealing with a foundation run by a professional staff—letters, phone calls, meetings, proposals—you have become an expert. No fooling.

15

Clichés, Chestnuts, and Caveats

Each of us looks at the world through his own lens, so it should come as no surprise when somebody doesn't see the same thing we do. Ambrose Bierce could describe a philanthropist as "a rich (and usually bald) old gentleman who has trained himself to grin while his conscience is picking his pocket," while Thoreau said, "Philanthropy is almost the only virtue which is sufficiently appreciated by mankind."

I know one man who gives $500,000 a year for opera (it's his passion); another who recently gave $17 million to a college; and a third who came into the office of a community campaign and took out twelve crumpled one-dollar bills from the pockets of his workman's clothes and gave them to me. He said he just wanted to do something for the project and didn't need a receipt.

And I know others from whom it is almost impossible to get a contribution for *anything*.

If you work for a good project long enough, you may become frustrated and angry at people who don't feel your cause is as worthy as you do. The Kidney Foundation doesn't raise as much money as the Muscular Dystrophy Association, Swarthmore doesn't raise as much as Princeton, and your group may not raise as much as something else you consider less important.

Your frustrations are easy to cure: All you have to do is look at your project, whatever it is, and think of how much you did for it without pay and maybe without anybody knowing about it but you.

★　★　★

And now some observations I have made in the past 40 years. Maybe one of them will be just the thing you have been looking for. If a few seem to contradict something I've said before, think about it. Fund raising is full of contradictions because it is, after all, an art, not a science. And different conditions can account for contradictions just as different conditions in your kitchen change your recipe—some people like garlic, some people don't.

★　★　★

Never ask a major contributor for advice on how to conduct your campaign unless you really want it. He'll give it to you, and if you don't follow it he could get mad. If you do follow it, it probably won't work.

★　★　★

If you're running a big-city campaign and a corporation offers to lend you one of its executives to work with you in lieu of a gift, ask for the money. You'll be better off more often than not.

★　★　★

If there is some way of getting the name of a major donor attached to your project, on a scholarship, for example, do it. You'll probably have his commitment for life.

★　★　★

When you talk to a prospect who tells you he gives most of his money to something you don't approve of, don't try to enlighten him. He'll resent being told he gave away money foolishly, or he won't believe you, and your project is not likely to benefit.

★ ★ ★

Philanthropy was not created for the benefit of philanthropists. They understand the concept better than you may think they do. You *as asker* may be more important than they as givers. Be bold.

★ ★ ★

Most organizations protect their contributors' lists as though they were the crown jewels. They think they have a moral obligation to keep the list secret. Some groups are afraid the people on their list will give to another charity and give less to theirs. Your contributor did not appoint you his guardian and protector. All he did was give you some money. Let him decide whether he wants to support another project too. Do you have the right to prevent him from learning about something important that could interest him?

★ ★ ★

You would be wise to know the pet charity of your prospect. He may ask you for a gift to his before he makes one to yours, and you should be prepared with an answer.

★ ★ ★

Psychologists suggest light blue may be the color people respond to best in a fund raising context.

★ ★ ★

Don't be afraid to go back to a prospect who hasn't given anything. You can't offend him into giving *less*, can you?

★ ★ ★

The man who suggests you need 1,000 contributions of $10 each for your $10,000 project.
A. Knows arithmetic.
B. Thinks he's given you a brilliant solution.
C. Won't give more than $10.

★ ★ ★

Never tell a prospect your organization might collapse without his help. He might let it. Nobody likes to think his money could go down the drain.

★ ★ ★

I've heard a board of a charity debate whether or not to accept a large, no-strings contribution from a man with a shady reputation. It took a clergyman to convince them the organization would not be contaminated if they accepted the check. The Quakers say their acceptance sanctifies the money.

★ ★ ★

Patience, persistence, determination, and doggedness are more valuable than brilliance and talent when negotiating for a government grant. Don't sit back waiting and praying after you send in your application. Get in there and talk to senators, congressmen, aides, secretaries, receptionists, elevator operators—anybody and everybody. It works.

★ ★ ★

People who say they haven't time to work on a worthwhile campaign never watched a child with muscular dystrophy trying to learn to walk.

★ ★ ★

If a celebrity offers to do a benefit for you free, don't think it won't cost you anything. You'll have to pay for transportation and expenses of the celebrity and maybe one or two others of his party, an accompanist or other musicians if he needs them, and other hidden costs that could make your free benefit an expensive performance.

★ ★ ★

Never schedule a meeting of any kind unless you know in advance what you want to accomplish. Nothing kills enthusiasm quicker than disorganization and drift.

★ ★ ★

If the featured speaker on your program drones on endlessly, fake a heart attack, or faint or scream. Do anything you can to stop him before he wrecks your meeting. Better still, give him a time limit in advance and insist he stick to it.

★ ★ ★

In families of great wealth, the founder of the fortune and his grandchild will usually be more generous than the generation in between.

★ ★ ★

If you are forced to make a choice between a widow and a widower of equal wealth, go after the widower. Most of the time you'll get more. Men are better prospects than women, with exceptions, of course. One obvious reason is that men usually feel they can continue to make money at their business or profession, while most women don't. Women, however, put in more time at fund raising than men do.

★ ★ ★

Doctors and lawyers, with some notable exceptions, are among the toughest prospects to solicit in a campaign.

★ ★ ★

Self-made men, merchants, and manufacturers are *usually* more generous than bankers, brokers, and insurance executives.

★ ★ ★

Mean, median, and mode are three different kinds of averages. Averaging can be useful to you in fund raising, so on the chance you don't know the differences among them, I'll explain.

Mean: You divide the total you raised by the number of gifts to find your mean average gift: $63,000 raised, 700 gifts, average gift $90. This is the averaging method used most often, but it may not always be best for the information you need.

Median: The gift that divides the list of givers in half; 350 gifts above the median and 350 gifts below the median.

Mode: The typical gift, the one you get most often. Of the 700 gifts in our example, let's say more people gave $150 than any other amount; $150 would be the mode average.

In fund raising the most useful average is usually the mode. When you review last year's figures you will get a clearer picture of your typical contributor by looking for the mode average. Then you can devise strategies to persuade that typical giver to increase his gift from $150 to perhaps $200. But if you used the mean average, you would be thinking about a $90 average giver. If you used the median, you would be figuring strategies for a handful of givers.

One unusually large gift can distort the mean average but will have no effect on the mode.

★ ★ ★

Usually, 90 percent of the money in a campaign comes from about 10 to 15 percent of the donors. So spend 90 percent of your time and effort on the few, as undemocratic as it may appear to be.

★ ★ ★

Fear is a greater force for giving than love.

★ ★ ★

It has been said that some people wouldn't go to Europe if they were forbidden to send postcards home. Similarly, there are some people who won't work on a fund drive unless their picture is in the paper at least once. If you need them badly enough, try to accommodate them. If you don't need them, forget it.

★ ★ ★

About 340 years ago a group of New Amsterdam settlers petitioned Director General Petrus Stuyvesant to allow a group of immigrants to land. They pledged their farms and fortunes so that the new immigrants would not become a charge on the community. It was probably the first community-wide drive in the New World.

★ ★ ★

The amount of money raised for political purposes should be the only evidence you need that tax deductions aren't the only reason people give money away.

★ ★ ★

You have to pass strict state and local tests before you can get a job as a barber. To become president of a million-dollar charity you don't even have to pass a reading test.

★　★　★

If every man, woman, and child in the United States sent you $1 and asked for a receipt in response to your fund raising letter, you'd spend more than you got.

★　★　★

There is no such thing as the right or wrong time of year or month to have a campaign. I have never heard anybody say *this* is the perfect time. When you have made your plans properly, it's the right time.

★　★　★

Some people who say they gave at the office really did. But you should check the records to make sure.

★　★　★

The National Foundation spent millions of dollars on research before it made a small grant to a relatively obscure doctor in Pittsburgh named Jonas Salk, who developed the polio vaccine. Do you need a better argument for giving to medical research projects?

★　★　★

Everybody thinks their city or club or neighborhood is different from all others when it comes to fund raising. They're wrong. Aside from easily learned local customs, every group is basically the same.

★　★　★

Don't let anybody talk you into mailing out useless gadgets with the hope that people will send back $5. Aside from being offensive, unbearably expensive, illegal in some places, and just short of blackmail, the only one who profits is the gadget-maker.

★ ★ ★

If you make vague promises or talk about vague objectives when discussing your project, you'll get vague pledges and vague checks.

★ ★ ★

On the average, a donor will usually leave about three times as much to his favorite organizations as he gave them while he was alive. But to be sure you get it, ask him about it while he's living.

★ ★ ★

Never call it Frisco or St. Looie. If you do and you're trying to raise money in those cities, pack up and go home. Abuse of local customs can ruin a campaign.

★ ★ ★

A community that supports more than one fund drive can usually afford another. They're like a family with several children that adopts another child. Nobody suffers, everybody benefits, because there's enough love to go around.

★ ★ ★

Any campaign that *must* have a brochure to explain it is too complicated for most donors. If yours is one, rethink it!

★ ★ ★

If your prospect says he can't give to your project because he's giving everything this year to dear old Tech, drop a polite note to the president of Tech. Tell him how delighted you are. Tech may not know about the intentions of your prospect and they'll owe you a favor. Tech may even try to help *you* if your prospect changes his mind about them.

★   ★   ★

Nobody ever sent a contribution to a billboard.

★   ★   ★

Don't send a form letter and a pamphlet about last wills and bequests to your members or alumni over sixty. Most of them will ignore it and some will cut you out if you're already in because you didn't treat them with kid gloves. While some people just won't talk about dying and writing a will, others will respond to a personal letter, carefully written, asking for an appointment.

★   ★   ★

People who get angry when asked to contribute to a worthy cause probably kick their dogs.

★   ★   ★

Some government and foundation grants are made on a matching basis—they'll give you a dollar for every dollar or two you raise yourself. Since everybody loves a bargain, try to use the matching gift idea with individual donors; you pledge to raise a dollar for every dollar they give up to an agreed total.

★   ★   ★

Nobody ever gave up a mink coat or a BMW because he gave too much money to the Heart Fund.

★   ★   ★

Nobody wants to be the only giver in a campaign, so always try to get as many smaller gifts as you can for balance—but don't spend more than 10 percent of your energies getting them.

★ ★ ★

When you plan your big fund raising dinner, leave out the soup. It will save you money; it will save about fifteen minutes for your program; the soup will probably be cold anyway; and if the crowd is big enough, somebody is bound to get soup dumped in his lap. Besides, wealthy prospects don't come to fund dinners just for the meal.

★ ★ ★

When you have your fund campaign dinner, count the number of waiters and the number of shrimp in the cocktails. There should be one waiter to ten guests, five jumbo or six medium shrimp per cocktail. At a major hotel dinner for five hundred people you could be taken for plenty and get lousy service and skimpy cocktails.

★ ★ ★

If you're having an event to which a hundred or more people have made reservations in advance, you can guess that 8 to 10 percent won't show up. It could be important to you if you have to guarantee a precise number for a dinner or lunch and pay for the guaranteed number. People catch colds, relatives come in unexpectedly from out of town, Junior falls off his bike and has to have his leg put in a cast, or something else comes up. Remember, 8 to 10 percent of *paid* ticket holders don't show.

★ ★ ★

When you arrange seating for a committee meeting or other gathering of fifty people or less, set up fewer chairs than you think you'll need. An empty chair at a meeting looks as though somebody was expected and didn't care enough to come. If you bring in extra chairs just before the meeting starts, it looks as though more people care than you thought.

★ ★ ★

At your dinner or luncheon you may be in a banquet room that can seat many more people than you're able to gather. Try to reserve a room that fits your expected crowd. Four hundred people in a room that holds five hundred will look like a bigger crowd than six hundred people in a room that can hold two thousand. If you're stuck in an oversized room, have the banquet manager move the tables one foot farther apart than his chart calls for. Then seat people at tables of eight rather than ten each.

★ ★ ★

Always assume your prospect has more money than your original estimate. You may be right or he may be flattered at your evaluation. In either case you could get more than you thought you would. Pitch high!

16

A Two-Minute Review

Robert Benchley is supposed to have said, "The world is divided into two groups. One group divides the world into two groups, the other doesn't."

In the world of fund raising there *are* two groups: One is made up of people like you who work on campaigns and the other is everybody else.

I've watched your group and worked with you and admired you. You often wonder what made you get involved in the first place but you stay with it. And we both know why: Your project is important, people depend on it and upon you to see it through. No campaign can exist without you and the other people in your group. If you decided to quit, every nonprofit organization in the country would have to close. They won't because you won't let them. And now that you know even more about fund raising than you did a few hours ago, there's no chance you'll quit because you want to try out a few new ideas. Right?

So let's take one last look at what you know:

- In a fund raising campaign the inner group must give first and give sacrificially.

- Take great care when you recruit the leaders of your campaign. They are your most important asset.

- Make the case for your project as human and brief as you can.

- Set a goal that makes sense; one that fits your project.

- Build your prospect list with care. Brainstorm.

- Do your homework—research your prospects.

- Rate your prospects and ask them for a *specific* amount.

- Don't expect publicity to raise money.

- Don't use a fund raising event or method *only* because you're afraid to ask for money eyeball to eyeball.

Remember my definition of the art of fund raising? You raise money when you ask for it, preferably face to face, from the smallest possible number of people, in the shortest period of time, at the least expense. If one thing sticks with you, I hope it's that definition, because you'll never learn anything more important about fund raising. In the definition, focus on *preferably face to face:* Everything I've said in these pages boils down to that. It's almost childishly simple, isn't it?

The late comic genius Ernie Kovacs once did a sketch about the launching of a huge ocean liner. The champagne bottle smashed against the prow, the ship slid gracefully into the water—and sank. Don't launch your campaign and sink it yourself. When everything is ready, don't suddenly change your mind because somebody tells you it's not the right time, or fund raising is uncouth, or you'll never get anywhere. They're wrong, and you'll be cheating yourself and your project if you believe them.

There was a time when writers addressed their readers as "gentle reader." I'm going to revive the practice, because you wouldn't be reading this unless you were working for a noble cause.

So, gentle reader, forget your inhibitions, look your prospect in the eye, ask for the gift to your campaign, and when he says, "How do I make out the check?" you will feel a sense of accomplishment I have never been able to describe. The feeling you have done something decent, worthwhile, and unselfish is a reward you will cherish all your life.

APPENDIX: EVENT CHECKLIST

Event	*Date & Time*	*Place*

☐ Budget
☐ Backward calendar
☐ Community calendar
   a. Clearance
   b. Notification
☐ Hotel or hall
☐ Guest of honor
☐ Chairman
☐ Co-chairmen
☐ Honorary chairman
☐ Women's chairman
☐ Talent
☐ Committee
   a. Letters for sponsors
   b. Committee named
   c. Assignments
   d. Report meetings
☐ Letterhead
☐ Mailing list
☐ First invitation
   a. Envelopes printed
   b. Envelopes addressed
   c. Invitation printed
   d. Reply cards
   e. Reply envelopes
   f. Signatures
☐ Second invitation

☐ Third invitation
☐ Advertising & publicity
   a. Newspaper
   b. Outdoor
   c. Radio-TV
☐ Awards and citations
☐ Pre-event meetings
☐ Special pledge cards
☐ Tickets
   a. Dinner tickets
   b. Special event tickets
☐ Phone squads
☐ Hotel reservations
☐ Airport reception
☐ Press conference
☐ Menu
☐ Minimum hotel guarantee
☐ Transportation
   a. Personnel
   b. Equipment
☐ Reception or cocktail party
   a. Room
   b. Invitation
   c. Phone squad
   d. Agenda
   e. Other

APPENDIX: EVENT CHECKLIST (*Cont'd*)

Event	Date & Time	Place

☐ Signs and banners
☐ Doormen and ushers
☐ Flowers and decorations
☐ Badges
☐ Hostesses
☐ Singer of national anthem
☐ Accompanist
☐ Piano
☐ Police
☐ Photographer
☐ Lights
☐ Sound-recording
☐ Kits
   a. Applications
   b. Literature
   c. Blank checks
   d. Receipt books
   e. Workers' pledges
☐ Agenda
   a. Speeches & introductions
   b. Invocation-benediction
☐ Fund raising
   a. Pre-event
   b. By ticket
   c. Open pledges
   d. Card calling

☐ Materials
   a. Pencils
   b. Clips
   c. Pads
   d. Staplers
   e. Flags
   f. Adding machine
   g. Rubber bands
   h. Easels
   i. Change
   j. Masking tape
   k. Displays
☐ Registration tables
☐ Head table place cards
☐ Seating charts
   a. Reservation lists
   b. Table assignment cards
☐ Wires from V.I.P.s
☐ Staff assignments
☐ Dressing room
☐ Thank-you letters
☐ Cash collections
   a. Mail
   b. Phone
☐ Complete File of Materials

Index

About the Author

Irving R. Warner brings over forty years of experience to *The Art of Fund Raising*. He has crisscrossed the North American continent from Vancouver to Miami, from Montreal to San Diego, guiding and counseling campaigns in seventy-two cities. His clients have been religious groups, public interest causes, private hospitals and health agencies, think tanks, colleges and universities. In this book he has distilled hundreds of campaigns involving thousands of people—super-rich to the just-getting-by. And because he started his career as a writer, he tells what he knows in clear, understandable language.

He is president of the Irving R. Warner Company, a Los Angeles-based consulting firm with clients in New York, Illinois, Kansas, Georgia, and Washington, D.C.